"I found this book, stimulating, insightful and helpful. Above all, I found it amusing and short, two crucial attributes lacking in most change books. It will certainly find a place on my bookshelf, and I would strongly recommend it to anyone interested or involved in change."

Bernard Burnes, *Stirling Management School, UK*

"What a wonderful contribution to the change management literature. A delightful yet thought provoking book that engages the reader from the start with cartoon images, accessible text and practical exercises. This welcome addition promotes thought and reflection on complex change issues and opens up multiple pathways for navigating and dealing with change."

Patrick Dawson, *University of Aberdeen, UK*

"Do you think the best way to implement change is to follow the steps in a textbook? Think again. Or, better still, join Richard and Brenda in Reimagining Change to discover a more liberating, inspiring, and creative approach that is visually stimulating, with provocative questions prompting you to think, feel, and act differently as a change agent."

David A. Buchanan, *Cranfield University, UK*

Reimagining Organizational Change

This engaging and thought-provoking book offers a rich, multifaceted approach to mastering leadership and driving organizational change. With its extensive, playful and insightful use of cartoons, thought-provoking debriefs, and practical self-assessments, the book is designed to be not only a guide but an experience, turning the often-complex topics of leadership and change into accessible, memorable images. Each chapter is filled with illustrations that not only lighten the mood but also provide deeper insights into the psychological and organizational dynamics at play in bringing about change.

At the heart of the book lies a comprehensive and dynamic 5M framework that reimagines the change process as the Mindful Mobilization of Maps, Masks and Mirrors. This framework is designed to challenge traditional approaches to change, offering fresh perspectives on how to navigate the often murky waters of organizational transformation.

Whether you are a student looking to navigate the complexities of organizational theory, a consultant seeking fresh strategies to introduce and communicate change or a lecturer hoping to inspire your students with innovative teaching methods, this book provides an entertaining, insightful and memorable resource and guide.

Richard J. Badham is a Professor of Management, and Adjunct Fellow at the University of Technology Sydney, Australia.

Brenda M. Santiago is a Managing Partner in the strategic change consultancy firm Inspiring Change Pty Ltd.

Routledge Focus on Business and Management

The fields of business and management have grown exponentially as areas of research and education. This growth presents challenges for readers trying to keep up with the latest important insights. *Routledge Focus on Business and Management* presents small books on big topics and how they intersect with the world of business research.

Individually, each title in the series provides coverage of a key academic topic, whilst collectively, the series forms a comprehensive collection across the business disciplines.

Evolution of the Global Fitness Industry
Strategy, Sustainability and Innovation
Patrizia Gazzola, Enrica Pavione and Francesco Ferrazzano

Digital Transformation of Performing Arts
Trends in the Classical Music Industry
Salvino A. Salvaggio

Globalization and Entrepreneurship
Cases from China, Japan and Bangladesh
Mirjana Radović-Marković, Yao Ouyang, and Md. Shajahan Kabir

Comparative Dynamics in the Comics Industry
Contrasting Cultures in France, Belgium and Netherlands
Rudi de Vries

Reimagining Organizational Change
Richard J. Badham and Brenda M. Santiago

For more information about this series, please visit: www.routledge.com/Routledge-Focus-on-Business-and-Management/book-series/FBM

Reimagining Organizational Change

Richard J. Badham and Brenda M. Santiago, with Jock Macneish

Routledge
Taylor & Francis Group
LONDON AND NEW YORK

First published 2025
by Routledge
4 Park Square, Milton Park, Abingdon, Oxon OX14 4RN

and by Routledge
605 Third Avenue, New York, NY 10158

Routledge is an imprint of the Taylor & Francis Group, an informa business

British Library Cataloguing-in-Publication Data
A catalogue record for this book is available from the British Library

ISBN: 978-1-032-62992-6 (hbk)
ISBN: 978-1-032-63001-4 (pbk)
ISBN: 978-1-032-62997-1 (ebk)

DOI: 10.4324/9781032629971

Typeset in Times New Roman
by SPi Technologies India Pvt Ltd (Straive)

Contents

Figures

Preface

On Cartoons

We use cartoons and imagery to make learning about change management and leadership more engaging and effective. Why cartoons? A picture paints a thousand words, but we can go further. Cartoons can simplify ideas, stimulate discussions, reduce stress, build emotional connections, and promote teamwork. Here's how they can help:

- **Simplify complex issues** by breaking down complicated concepts into simpler visuals.
- **Increase engagement** since humour and relatable images can make learning more fun.
- **Encourage critical thinking** by using visuals that can spark discussions. Analysing a cartoon about leadership situations can stimulate thinking about different perspectives and deepen understanding.
- **Reduce cognitive load** by presenting images that inform without further burdening a student or practitioner overwhelmed with the amount and complexities of change management Information.
- **Build emotional connections** by showing the human side of change, such as feelings of resistance or adaptation. These emotional connections help people better understand the challenges others face during change.
- **Encourage collaboration and improve communication skills** by encouraging groups to work together to analyse cartoons, encouraging teamwork.

The cartoons in this book are humorous reminders of what we do wrong and provide insightful visuals to help remind and guide us on what to do better. We live in a world where top-down 'rational instructions from higher up' do not solve the problem. Far more entertaining and compelling is the use of humour and parody that causes us to reflect on our fallibilities and follies. We use cartoons to gently prod us into creating a better version of ourselves and greater success at work.

Who Is This Book For?

This book provides inspirational, amusing and practical support for all those caught in the throes of change, change consultants and facilitators, lecturers and students of change.

How might you use this book?

1. As a general reader who wants to get things done but often finds it difficult, then it is a fun, helpful resource for insight and inspiration. The self-deprecating humour in the cartoons may lighten your day and reduce your tension when confronting the challenges of change. The memorable imagery is a playful reminder of the realities of change to help prevent us from repeating our mistakes. Each cartoon and section can be enjoyed. If you are stimulated, we encourage you to explore the framework and relevant readings that inform them.
2. As a change manager or consultant, the cartoons, explanations and tests can each be used as stand-alone bases for stimulating thought and discussion amongst those driving, experiencing or impacted by the change. Many of you apply standard methodologies (e.g., the PROSCI ADKAR model) or staged approaches in change programmes and projects. You can use the book for accessible, humorous and stimulating ways to illustrate your message and as an informative and stress-reducing self-help playbook.
3. As a lecturer or student of managing or leading change, the cartoons can lighten up course material, foster open or guided reflection on key change issues, and provide memorable illustrations and reminders of what a proactive change mindset involves. Each cartoon provides succinct and emotive illustrations of issues we would all do well to remember – and enjoy ourselves.
4. As a lecturer, consultant or simply someone interested in self-development, the book can be a light and easy introduction to a systematic approach to understanding and influencing change. Our textbook *Ironies of Organisational Change* (2023) delves into this approach and informs the free online Coursera *course Leading Transformations. Manage Change*. Further details on this course and text and how the cartoons, explanations, and tests are aligned with them are provided in the *Introduction* and at the end of each section. It includes how the cartoons inform and are informed by two other books of ours on change: *Power, Politics and Organizational Change* co-authored with Dave Buchanan (Sage, 2020) and *Short Change* (Business Perspectives, Amazon Kindle, 2014).

The cartoons in this book are stimulated by and support a perspective on change that has inspired over 4,000 senior and middle managers to lead change more effectively. Our advice is to use the pictures and images, advice on their use and the self-tests to:

- Reflect on how you and others currently think and act,
- Inspire you to make improvements and decide what to focus on, and
- Consider using these cartoons to inspire and keep these changes in mind.

Let's look at an example.

The contrast between management and leadership is a common yet contested topic. Targets and Dreams highlights one feature: the difference between instructing people to achieve goals and inspiring them to realize an aspirational purpose. It captures the intellectual component, the feelings generated, and the symbolic body language embedded within.

Think About It

Figure 0.1, Targets and Dreams, gives an apparently simple yet visually suggestive insight into the differences between managing and leading change. Note how the manager's speech bubble on the left states, 'You

Figure 0.1 Targets and Dreams.

have a target', a command from 'on high', instructing what 'you' have to do. The top-down finger points at a burdened and worried 'employee' holding a financial ($) report. The leader's speech bubble on the right, 'We have a dream' (with the dream emphasized), is an uplifting message to someone on the same level, symbolized by the up-turned palm. The employee seems happy, smiling, motivated, and maybe even inspired with animated hand gestures.

How might you use Targets and Dreams to stimulate discussion and reflection on managing and leading change? As a source of personal reflection, or as a lecturer or consultant, you might use the cartoon to focus on how people feel as well as think when they are delivered 'target' or 'dream' messages (there might be other, even opposing, views than that expressed in the cartoon). You might also think about individual and organizational 'body language'. How might you read 'management' or 'leadership' approaches and their impacts on how messages are delivered, including medium, tone, venue, direction of communication, how punishment and rewards are allocated, and physical 'body language' itself? This can then encourage discussion on how an effective change agent might address such factors in setting and communicating direction.

We hope this has piqued your interest enough for you to begin the journey with us. Have fun along the way, and good luck!

Acknowledgements

To all those who have amused and instructed us in the way they bring humour, laughter, fun and tears to reflections on life and work. While there are so many we are indebted to, we would like to particularly acknowledge the singular character, sense of irony and playfulness of (alphabetically) Adam Attar, Fernando Sulsona Santiago, Hazel England, Ian McLoughlin, Julians (Woodbridge and Laing), Mark Finsterer, Michael Zanko, Pedro Cardona Roig and Yehudi Webster. Our special thanks and gratitude go to Jock Macneish, our professional cartoonist at Strategic Images. His creative translation of the key ideas into fun and insightful cartoons was invaluable. Without him, the book would not have been possible.

Introduction

This short book provides an image-laden view of how we routinely mislead change and what we might do about it. It is common knowledge that we do not manage change well and do not seem to learn from our mistakes. To help address this problem, Reimagining Change provides a new framework for thinking about change and a playbook of fun cartoons to illustrate it.

The book has three main sections, each with its role. At the end of each section, key takeaways and references are summarized and direct you to additional support materials. The recommendations for additional reading refer you to overviews found on our website, Coursera program and relevant chapters in our key books on change. These resources offer an accessible introduction to what can be a complex and often dense body of literature.

Our website, Reimagining Change (www.reimaginingchange.com), contains valuable free resources, including a brief (2.5-minute) video that introduces Reimagining Change and previews what can be found in the companion volume to this book, *Ironies of Organizational Change* (Badham and Santiago, 2023). Additionally, the website also contains supplementary material to *Coursera's Online MOOC Program: Leading Transformations: Manage Change* (Coursera.org) and shows how you can enrol in this program for free, earn a certificate, and learn new skills.

The main accompanying texts are:

- Badham, R. and Santiago, B. (2023), *Ironies of Organizational Change* (Elgar, London). Available in hard copy and soft copy on Google Play. Further annotated readings are to be found at the end of each chapter.
- Coursera's *Online MOOC Program*: '*Leading Transformations: Manage Change*' Access for free, instructions on the Reimagining Change website. The course provides video lectures, readings, and additional tests that cover each chapter of this book. Further annotated readings are found at the end of each week.

- Badham, R. (2014), *Short Change: An Introduction to Managing Change* (Business Perspectives, Suny). Available on Kindle. This brief introduction provides you with short accessible chapters on each of the components of the 5M Framework.
- Buchanan, D. and Badham, R., (1999, 2008, 2020), *Power, Politics and Organizational Change* (Sage, London) Available in hard copy and soft copy on Kindle. This provides, in particular, useful background information for Chapters 5–8.

Section 1 An Invitation to Change

The invitation is to open your mind and reimagine change in a new way. Defining the real problem lies at the heart of creating useful solutions. Replacing established habits and images with new and more useful ones is essential. *An Invitation to Change* redefines the change problem as the gap between our aspirations and achievements and how we routinely mislead ourselves and others by failing to address the reasons for this.

We reimagine ourselves and our organizations as 'icebergs' and our change journey as a 'rollercoaster' ride. These simple and memorable metaphors provide a new way of thinking about this change problem and our solution.

Our invitation concludes by presenting an accessible and creative '5M' framework that supports you in reimagining change into a practical and enjoyable process for bringing change about.

Figure 0.2 illustrates the journey you are invited to embark upon. The old view of change as a rigid two-step process of implementing a new

Figure 0.2 The Infinite Journey.

order is replaced by a more fluid 'infinity' view of change as a continuous and never-ending process.

Think About It

Each change journey is viewed differently and raises different issues for the participants. Note in Figure 0.2 the person out front pointing forward and holding the banner, the person at the end looking back and perspiring, and the doubt, confusion and pointing by the jumbled crowd in between. Does this capture something of the chaos and frustration you experience in change?

How might you use Figure 0.2, The Infinite Journey, as a thought-provoking invitation to look at change and your role in it differently?

Section 2 Cycle of Change

Managing or leading change initiatives requires understanding and skill in planning what to do, fulfilling the planned tasks and monitoring and adjusting actions along the way. In traditional project management terms, success in these areas creates a productive 'plan-do-check' cycle.

Reimagining Change goes beyond a traditional project management view of the change cycle. As outlined in the first part of the '5M' framework, this involves *mapping* out a complex journey, donning *masks* and giving performances and creatively deploying *mirrors* to help learn and adapt along the way.

This section assists you in preparing for, executing and adjusting your change initiative by reimagining the change process as an iterative cycle of Maps, Masks and Mirrors.

Section 3 Leading Change

The change cycle often stalls. Knowing what should be done is one thing; getting it done is quite another. Leadership in change is all about being aware of the challenges and proactively addressing them.

The two key capabilities are being *mindful* of barriers and complexities and *mobilizing* energy, resources and support to address these challenges. The disposition required is a *lightness of being*. This section assists you in understanding and experimenting with a key component of reimagining change: reinventing yourself as a leader.

Managing change is the discipline of influencing yourself and other people to achieve a purpose. The 5M framework (elaborated in Sections 2 and 3) assists you by capturing what is involved as the *Mindful Mobilizing of Maps, Masks and Mirrors*. Figure 0.3 captures this framework by presenting the 5M Change Cycle as a wheel of Maps, Masks and Mirrors and Leading Change as a Mindful and Mobilizing cyclist.

Figure 0.3 The 5M Framework.

Think About It

As illustrated by the image of the cyclist, a key component of change is maintaining a productive change cycle. Like the cyclist, exercising leadership involves an energetic balancing act that requires mindful adjustments in direction, navigating obstacles, and powering up the cycle to make this possible.

How might you use Figure 0.3 to assess how well you or others handle change? Reflect on how much time and skill are dedicated to each of the five activities: the Mindful Mobilizing of Maps, Masks and Mirrors.

In Conclusion

We emphasize the importance of adopting a seriously playful approach to change as highlighted in this playbook of creative and insightful images. Reimagining change is grounded on three key principles: redefining the change problem, creating a productive change cycle and becoming a leader of change.

Section 1

An Invitation to Change

1 The Change Problem

Einstein was onto something! Conventional approaches to change management try to solve the problem of change by using the same tools that created the situation in the first place. They provide you with designs to implement designs and strategies for executing strategies but there is often little effect. Why? Individuals and organizations face an inherent gap between their aspirations and achievements. The gap widens when organizations aspire to innovate but have ingrained cultures and practices that hinder their achievement. In failing to appreciate and effectively address this gap fully, conventional change management becomes part of what we term 'the change problem'. In this chapter, we introduce you to how thinking inside the box of conventional change management misleads change, the risks of change and the dangers of conformity, the chaos and biases that make achieving change so challenging, and the importance of pulling rather than pushing change.

The image of the change management box below parodies the conventional approach of project management or business-as-usual to handling the challenges of change. Conventional approaches to change management provide a prescriptive toolbox of actions and checklists. See, for example, Prosci's ADKAR model or the courses and certifications from the Project Management Institute and leading consultancies (Prosci, 2024; Project Management Institute, 2024). These provide useful initial guidelines about likely stages of change, key issues to be confronted and standard advice for change experts on the actions to take. However, they often ignore or underestimate the uncertainty, complexity, emotion and politics that lie 'outside the box'.

Think About It

Figure 1.1, The Box, pictures a 'traditional' character, suit and tie in place, making a bit of a splash paddling in the change management pool. He is forced to go in circles as his efforts are tightly bound by the walls of the

DOI: 10.4324/9781032629971-2

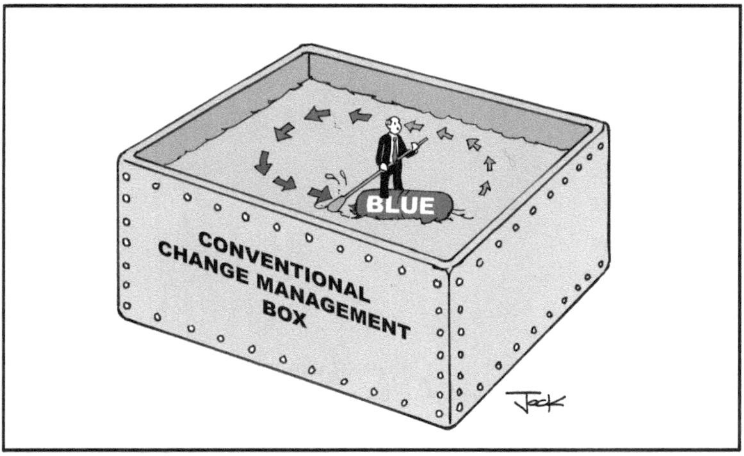

Figure 1.1 The Box.

change management 'tool' box. He may even be rudderless. His only 'boat' is a Blue Pill, a reference to the staid, conventional, yet misleading view of the world presented to the character Leo (played by Keanu Reeves) in the movie *The Matrix*.

Are you or your organization tempted to address the uncertainties and anxieties of change by imposing rules and controls? Do you find the same-old, same-old advice on offer that doesn't stick and doesn't capture the complexity and barriers, the mess, and the politics of real-world change? Do you suspect that change experts are more concerned with the success of the operation (filling out the boxes) than whether the patient survives (achieving sustainable change)?

How does Figure 1.1 help you capture and communicate the restricted nature of this view of change management? How important is our admission of this reality, and how might we take action to avoid it?

As individuals and organizations, we often fail to bring about the changes we had planned and hoped for. The traditional change management cliché is that strategic changes fail 70% of the time (Badham and Santiago, 2023). The figure is highly contentious. Yet, the reality of our achievements rarely matches our aspirations. How often do we fail to properly consider the real challenges of turning our dreams into reality? The cartoon below parodies the disastrous consequences of blindly following what the masses do. Suppose we do what we, as individuals and organizations, usually do. In that case, the chances are that we will suffer the same fate as so many others: failure to achieve objectives, with costs ranging from wasting time, effort and resources to real damage to ourselves, our careers and those we were trying to 'change'.

To illustrate this point, Figure 1.2 uses the popular image of lemmings following each other over the precipice.

Figure 1.2 100,000 Lemmings Can't Be Wrong.

Think About It

Figure 1.2, 100,000 Lemmings Can't Be Wrong, pokes fun at those who simply follow others as they stick to unthinking conventions. The overlooked warning sign that notes a '70% failure' rate symbolizes the harsh realities of change that often prevent desired changes from being realized. The question mark (?) following the statistic highlights the contentious nature of relying solely on numerical 'evidence'.

Have you and others experienced the pressure to conform to established methods of change, even when this has not worked well? Do you, yourself, often want to 'hurry up and do it' despite past experiences of things going disastrously wrong? Does your organization rely on traditional, overly rational, control-oriented, and analytical approaches to change because they fit the managerial ethos – often due to cost?

How might you use Figure 1.2 as a mindful reminder and a warning of the dangers of failing to view change differently?

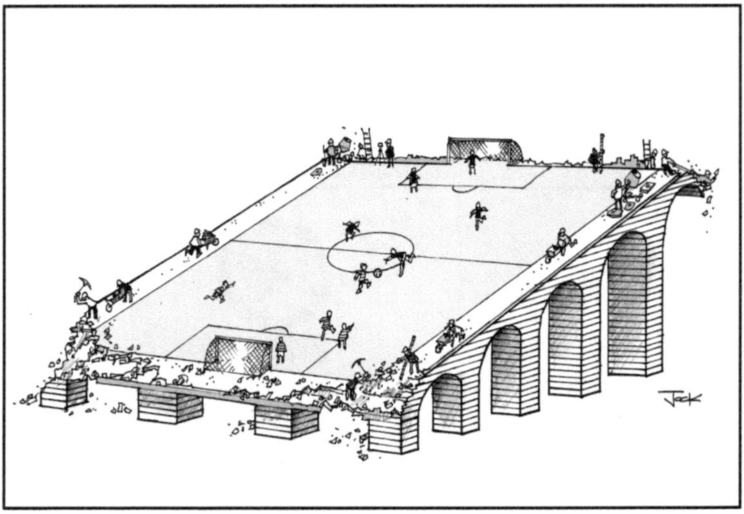

Figure 1.3 It's Not a Level Playing Field.

Figure 1.3, 'It's Not a Level Playing Field' presents the context of a chaotic soccer pitch, underscoring that how we make decisions is far less rational than we like to think. James March, the guru's guru, likened it to a round soccer field with several referees, numerous balls thrown into and off the field, and many goals (see Badham, 2022). We came across one manager in a well-known multinational who said their 'Goalposts change so often that they ought to have wheels on them!' It is difficult to succeed in achieving strategic change in such an environment.

The field of change is also far from level. We live in an organizational world in which the overemphasis on 'the head' (the rational) means the very real demands of 'the heart' (the emotional) are ignored or underemphasized. Designs are often not implemented. Strategies are not successfully executed. Being seen to initiate reforms is more important than effectively checking results. Routines become rituals, habits are difficult to overcome, and vested interests view change as a threat.

Think About It

Figure 1.3, It's Not a Level Playing Field, shows tattered goals, disorganized players, disruptive repairs and destructive reconstructions. Does this chaos and disorder above reflect your work experiences and how your organization changes? Have you felt that trying to change things is a frustrating and thankless uphill struggle? Do you yearn for simple goals and rules but find yourself swamped by ambiguity, competing agendas and agonising choices you do not want to make?

How might you use Figure 1.3 to help surface the chaos and biases you are facing or are likely to face and brainstorm how to handle the frustrations and challenges they create?

Figure 1.4 Push or Pull Change.

As individuals and organizations, we tend to 'push' change. Convinced we are right and tempted to tell it how it is, we issue instructions to 'just do it'. This could be called the 'Nike approach to managing change'. Under pressure, we also tend to go into 'fight and flight' mode when trying to change the situation and remove the problem. We lash out aggressively, bark commands, shout, avoid, and run away.

People don't like 'being changed', particularly when unwanted. If the changes require effort, require doing things they would rather not do, upset accustomed habits, and push people outside their comfort zones, then the response is predictable. Much like the effect of pushing a forcefield, there is pushback.

There is another way. Work on 'pulling' change by motivating those required to change. Find out what would stop people from changing, and work with them to remove the obstacles. Identify and work with people's needs and interests to mobilize their energy to overcome any reluctance to change. Address the heart as well as the head. Foster hope and enthusiasm or tap into insecurities and fears so that people 'want to change'. The image on the right illustrates how it can all seem so easy and natural when people are involved and 'pull together'.

Think About It

Do you identify with the left side of Figure 1.4, 'Push or Pull Change'? The 'boss' himself is part of the problem. He's barking instructions to uninterested or shocked employees. Note the perspiration of the employee pushing change uphill all alone, with 'cobwebs' symbolizing the 'sticky' nature of the enterprise. Have you had any experience of the surprising ease and the managers as bystanders when people are motivated to change like the one on the right hand of Figure 1.4?

How might you use Figure 1.4 as a simple and motivating reminder of the unproductive temptation to 'instruct' and 'push' change and a stimulus for thinking about ways to motivate people to change?

Chapter 1 Self-Test

Select the <u>one best answer</u> that completes the statements below. There are several 'half-truths' in the other options to choose from. These capture something important but are misleading if taken too far. The 'correct answers' are in Appendix 1. If your answer is incorrect, you might reflect on how it may be 'half-right' but 'half-wrong'.

1. **Managing change is about**

   A. effective project management by 'ticking off' the change actions to be done at every stage of change.
   B. not being a 'pill' when trying to get people to change.
   C. working informally to get people to 'want' to change.
   D. influencing people by working with and going beyond change management checklists.

2. **When preparing for change, I tend to**

   A. determine what needs to be done and rely on my authority to tell people what to do.
   B. follow established methods and guidelines for managing change projects.
   C. be aware of and/or seek information on possible challenges and barriers and work with others to address them best.
   D. have a nagging worry about unforeseen problems, but I hope things will turn out OK.

3. **Change projects will succeed**

   A. if the goals are desirable and clearly communicated.
   B. less than one-quarter of the time.

C. when actions are taken to create readiness and overcome resistance, and fortune favours you.
D. if people think for themselves rather than simply following others.

4. **My change projects failing to achieve their objectives**

A. is not an option for me.
B. is something I am wary of, and I seek to identify and address possible barriers.
C. is something that only happens if I make mistakes.
D. is highly likely, so I work on stories of how to blame others.

5. **The energy for change comes from**

A. my enthusiasm and commitment alone; without that, I won't inspire others or persevere over time.
B. significant others not from me.
C. pushing people to move outside their comfort zones.
D. mobilizing myself and a supportive coalition by enrolling diverse views and interests.

6. **When seeking a change in myself or others, I**

A. work on capturing and aligning real motivation and removing major obstacles.
B. focus on selling an inspiring vision that makes people want to change.
C. concentrate on overcoming complacency and creating urgency by building burning platforms.
D. believe, if I am honest, that if people can be shown the benefits of change, it will just happen.

2 Reimagining Change, Reinventing Yourself

In an important sense, you already know what is necessary to manage change. Yet, we often fail to attend to what we know. We default reflexively to established overly rational views of what change involves or should involve. In this sense, reimagining change is akin to breaking a habit. To help kick this habit, this chapter introduces two counter-images as sources of inspiration and powerful reminders. These are the organization as an Iceberg and the change journey as a Rollercoaster. In addition, we invite you to reinvent yourself because reimagining change is also a personal challenge. It involves getting 'out of your head' and overcoming counter-productive reflex responses to irrationality and threat.

In Ancient Rome, Janus was a two-faced god of beginnings and ends, entrances and exits, changes, transitions, gateways, doorways and archways. Figure 2.1, Faces of Change, symbolizes the acceptance and creativity needed to adopt multiple masks since we must learn to think and act in different, often opposing, ways.

Individuals and organizations have well-established 'formal faces'. They are forward-looking, rational and strategic. They are also the intuitive and attractive images we must display, at least in public. To some extent, however, they are artificial. They ignore much of what we know, and experience of how real-world organizations operate and transform. In a sense, we have an equally easily recognized 'informal face' that appreciates such matters. This face observes and communicates the conflicts, uncertainties and disorganization that hinder many change initiatives. It is realistic and resonates with experience. Yet, it can be dispiriting and self-fulfilling in its pessimism.

Reimagining change does not mean ignoring or totally abandoning the rational and strategic image of organizations and the need to confirm and conform to this image. What it does do, however, is recognize its partial nature and the dangers of taking this image as the only one. The Iceberg and the Rollercoaster images are designed to capture the formal and informal views of change and emphasize the importance of the informal one.

DOI: 10.4324/9781032629971-3

Figure 2.1 Faces of Change.

They highlight and prompt us to remember the tensions between our different images. They assist us in acknowledging and working with our embedded rational hopes and expectations while accepting and grappling with the emotions, politics and chaos that undermine them.

Think About It

Reimagining change acknowledges the existence of formal and informal, frontstage and backstage, orderly and disorderly, rational/strategic and emotional/political images of change. Reinventing yourself involves acknowledging the presence of these contrasting images, the importance of keeping them in mind and displaying an appreciation of both. Anyone managing and leading change has to look in two different directions, address two aspects of reality and handle two faces – like Janus!

How might you use Figure 2.1, Faces of Change, to encourage reflection and discussion on these different images of change and what is required to acknowledge them? Do you find the tensions between them difficult to handle? What does this say about how you might reinvent yourself?

In the popular mind, icebergs have a specific connotation. The image directs our attention to the mass hidden beneath the surface. Influenced by the story of the Titanic, the image highlights the threat posed by restricting our view to the less substantial 'tip' and failing to consider the dangers of neglecting the bulk below. Viewing organizations as icebergs focuses our mind on what lies underneath the formal public view of organizations as strategic rational enterprises. It highlights the dangers of paying insufficient attention to the informal, the emotion and chaos, the politics and the complexities of organizational life.

Figure 2.2 The Iceberg.

Figure 2.2, The Iceberg, acknowledges the visibility and attention given to the formal frontstage and rational 'tip' of organizational change while emphasizing the substantial importance, life and diversity of the bulk of backstage activities beneath the surface.

Think About It

In Figure 2.2, the sailor at the prow of the formal change vessel pushes the visible 'tip', seemingly without any insight into or consideration of the bulk below. The snorkellers, however, are looking at both the surface tip and the mass below. This means attending to the rational strategic tip and also having insight into the large mass and the crucial role of what lies beneath. It includes the informal politics, emotional challenges and complex uncertainties of change. These are often less obvious, frequently hidden and neglected at our peril.

The image also highlights the teeming life within and around icebergs in nature. Far from being the static, frozen blocks they first appear to be, Icebergs are alive and changing, in a continuous state of transformation in their lengthy journeys. Similarly, real-world organizations, unlike the image given by superficial stakeholder analyses and cultural surveys, are multi-levelled and shifting, with complex and uncertain dynamics. When describing and first analysing any change, how much time and thought do you spend on its formal, rational, strategic nature and rationale? In comparison, how far do you initially attend to the informal, emotional and political components and challenges? How often has it been a case of 'too little, too late' addressing these issues?

How might you use Figure 2.2, The Iceberg, to challenge assumptions and surface imbalances in what is prioritized during a change initiative? To what extent are those advocating for change, like sailors, merely pushing the tip of the iceberg? What important aspects of change are represented by the larger mass and the vibrant life beneath the surface? Additionally, what skills and abilities do the 'snorkellers' possess that allow them to view both the visible and hidden elements of change?

Figure 2.3 The Rollercoaster.

Our overly analytical mind likes to view change as a two-step rational process. The world 'as is' is problematic. Change ends this situation. It is a shift into a superior and healthy 'to be' state of affairs. Our attention is focused on 'what must be done'. Far less attention is paid to 'what needs to be done to get there'. It ignores the physical, mental and emotional states that people go through and must address in change.

In reaction, it is popular to recommend seeing change more realistically as a three-step transition: a challenging phase of separating from the past and dismantling the status quo; going through a difficult transitional process of handling anxieties and persisting in the face of hidden complexities and unexpected barriers; and, finally, entering a phase of embedding the change, avoiding the danger of slipping back into old ways.

Viewing the change journey as a rollercoaster ride builds on yet further develops and energizes this perspective on change. Rather than a fixed set of project stages or one three-step change process, change is viewed as an ongoing set of ups and downs. It blends excitement and anxiety. It contains rapid, stimulating, yet unnerving downhill runs. It also involves maintaining momentum through the bottom of a cycle and during effortful straining uphill climbs. Then on again to the next challenge.

Think About It

In Figure 2.3, the emotional rollercoaster ride is captured in the images of the riders, fretful and perspiring, joyous and excited, stuck and depressed, sweating and straining, and welcoming the new. When taken to heart, one of the relieving benefits of viewing change as a rollercoaster ride is accepting it is natural and 'all-right' to pass through various emotional states of anxiety and excitement, certainty and uncertainty, depression and overwhelm, tempered resilience and sense of thrilling achievement.

Reflect on any personal or work change you have initiated or been involved in. To what degree did you find yourself and others going through an emotional rollercoaster of optimism and hope followed by frustration and depression, only to have your hopes raised and possibly even dashed again? Did you find yourself and others 'clinging onto the sides' of your change vehicle, anxious and reluctant to let go in frightening conditions? Did this lead to counter-productive responses to uncertainties and threats?

How might the images and characters in Figure 2.3, The Rollercoaster, be used to encourage reflection on these issues? Could you spark discussion about the various emotions and stages of change by examining each of the five characters? Do the first two female characters represent a constructive response to the challenges of change, while the first two male characters represent the opposite?

Our instinct in modern culture is to use our heads at the expense of our hearts. We think a change is desirable and necessary; we point it out to others and expect action to follow. However, the status quo may be deeply embedded in difficult-to-change habits. Pursuing the change may be costly and difficult. Our 'good idea' may be met with denial, anger, disbelief, lethargy, fear of letting go/feeling awkward/things getting worse before they get better. The idea that achieving change requires persuasion and the deft exercise of influence to overcome such problems is not what many give thought to.

Then, there is also a default to a 'fight or flight' response when under pressure and threat. It is an automatic response of those required to change if they perceive it imposes costs. As initiators of a change, we perceive it to be obvious and desirable, and we respond to their resistance in a similarly dysfunctional way. The result is a downward fight/flight spiral of mutual recrimination.

Finally, we often respond to uncertainty and insecurity by rigidly adhering to outdated assumptions and plans, fearful of letting go and even doubling our dogmatic commitments. 'Release' can be scary, but it is also therapeutic and creative.

Think About It

Figure 2.4, Manage Yourself, depicts a manager confronted by a hand puppet that represents inner guidance. While contemplating his options, his one hand remains poised with a pen, stuck in his routine behaviour. Yet, to cope with and successfully handle the challenges of change, we must listen to our hand-puppet. We need to unlearn bad habits that contribute to our failures. This means becoming mindful of our tendencies to

Figure 2.4 Manage Yourself.

live too much in our heads and respond to threats with fight or flight responses. We need to learn to motivate ourselves and others to overcome these habits. This can be challenging and stressful. Note the manager's shocked expression and visible sweating. Yet developing such an awareness is essential given the challenges, uncertainties and tensions that arise from change and the strategies required to navigate them.

How often have you felt disappointed and discouraged by unforeseen costs or unexpected events in personal projects or workplace change initiatives? How well have you responded to unanticipated backlash, opposition and recrimination when attempting to bring about a change you believe is beneficial?

Have you found yourself disappointed and dispirited by attempts to improve yourself (lose weight, keep fit, improve your sporting skills, implement New Year's resolutions)? Have you experienced unexpected kick-back, opposition and recrimination when trying to influence others or an organization to bring about a change you believe is obviously desirable?

How can you use Figure 2.4, Manage Yourself, to promote reflection and discussion about improving your personal change capabilities? What insights does your personal 'hand puppet' reveal about areas where you need to improve? What fears and concerns about changing do you and others experience, as illustrated by the shocked expression and perspiration of the manager? What might you do about this?

Chapter 2 Self-Test

Select the <u>one best answer</u> that completes the statements below. There are several 'half-truths' in the other options to choose from. These capture something important but are misleading if taken too far. The 'correct answers' are in Appendix 1. If your answer is incorrect, you might reflect on how it may be 'half-right' but 'half-wrong'.

1. **Reimagining change means**

   A. focusing all our attention on politics and emotion in change.
   B. showing the public, frontstage and formal view of change as a lie.
   C. counter-balancing an over-reliance on strategic-rational images of change by including and emphasizing more messy-emotive images.
   D. rethinking change as an inherently desirable win-win development.

2. **The conventional image of change recommends that we should see change as**

   A. something negative we should resist.
   B. a strategic, rationally planned and controlled enterprise.

C. something we cannot influence or stop.
D. as messy, emotive and conflictual.

3. **When considering a change, I should**

A. focus my attention on the rational stuff, not interests and feelings.
B. spend most of my time and effort on what to do and much less on how to do it.
C. define a clear goal and develop a plan to get there.
D. iteratively adapt objectives and plans and align stakeholders with them.

4. **During a change, I**

A. focus on the 'hard' brief of achieving the task at hand, not the 'soft' chore of attending to feelings.
B. expect and prepare for the worst and make people aware of the barriers.
C. get excited by the opportunities and focus on communicating this to others.
D. prepare for and persevere through the highs and lows for me and others.

5. **My initial response to change should be to**

A. immediately find out exactly what this means for me and then consider others.
B. prepare myself and others to enjoy or at least work on making the most out of a likely bumpy ride.
C. focus my attention on supporting and comforting people through the pain.
D. concentrate on creating optimism about the change and fuelling hopes for a better future.

6. **When confronted by problems, dilemmas and opposition, I should**

A. calm myself and focus on solutions.
B. get tense and make instant decisions.
C. compromise and adapt.
D. lash out or give up and withdraw.

3 The 5M Framework

Managing change is not a separate speciality or the province of certified experts but an essential component of all our lives and the everyday work of managers and leaders. *It is the discipline of influencing yourself and other people to achieve a purpose*. It is about making change happen and achieving success by turning dreams, aspirations and obligations into reality. It is a discipline because many reflex reactions to our challenges are counter-productive. Rather than instructing, we need to build energy and enhance motivation. Rather than being dogmatic and aggressive, we must be open, mindful, inclusive, and engaging. Viewing this discipline as the *Mindful Mobilizing of Maps, Masks and Mirrors* reinforces this understanding and contains concepts and methods to guide and support your journey. This chapter introduces you to this perspective. The 5M Framework is an open and generative approach to change that informs and is illustrated and supported by cartoons, explanations and advice.

The 5M framework (Badham and Santiago, 2023; Inspiring Change, 2024) is deceptively simple and surprisingly memorable. It is a *framework for action* designed to help support and motivate those managing or leading change. It has two components. It views the change process as a *Cycle of Change* and *Leading Change* as the capabilities and disposition required to keep a productive Cycle of Change going.

The *Cycle of Change* is an ongoing iterative process reminiscent of the conventional Plan-Do-Check cycle project and operations managers use. The 5M Framework builds on and extends the traditional cycle by viewing 'Planning' as a more creative and fluid process of *Mapping* a journey, the 'Doing' of change as the donning of *Masks* in the performance of influence and 'Checking' as the creation and use of *Mirrors* to inform reflection and adaptation on the journey.

Leading Change is needed to keep the change cycle in motion. The importance of this task is not to be underestimated. The ideal Cycle of Change often faces disruptions and practical challenges. As one manager candidly said, 'We don't need more change management. We have plenty

DOI: 10.4324/9781032629971-4

of that, but nothing changes. What we need is 'DO management.' This underscores the importance of proactive action in the change process. The 5M Framework identifies those Leading Change as needing to be *Mindful* (of the gaps, complexities and barriers that hinder real-world change processes) and able and willing to *Mobilize* energy and support to overcome the challenges of change (motivating, building and maintaining coalitions and working with power and politics).

The 5M Framework brings together the *Cycle of Change* and *Leading Change*, addressing change management and leadership as the *Mindful Mobilizing of Maps, Masks and Mirrors.*

Figure 3.1 The Discipline.

Think About It

Figure 3.1 represents the 5M view of managing and leading change as a change cycle and cyclist. Progress is made by the turning of a change wheel guided and energized by the change cyclist. The change wheel continuously rotates in a cycle of orienting, performing and reflecting. This is the Maps-Masks-Mirrors cycle. The change cyclist gives the direction, energy and balance needed to keep the change wheel rotating and on track. These are the Mindful Mobilizing capabilities and disposition of the change leader.

How might you use Figure 3.1, The Discipline, to stimulate reflection and discussion on the process used in change initiatives and the capabilities and disposition of change leaders? What factors facilitate or prevent a 'wheel' from turning? Can you think of images or metaphors to represent the challenges that need to be addressed? What might facilitate or oppose each ' turn ' if you view the wheel as rotating through maps, masks and mirrors? Additionally, what makes a good cyclist? Can you use your answers as images or metaphors for what is needed from a change leader? How do these qualities relate to being mindful of barriers and complexity while also mobilizing energy and support?

Figure 3.2 Sisyphus and the 5M.

In Ancient Greek Mythology, Sisyphus was a king who angered the gods and was condemned to push a boulder up a hill only for it to roll back down again and repeat this for eternity. Renowned for his trickery, he was punished for his hubris. In the twentieth century, the French writer and philosopher Albert Camus (2023) introduced the idea of a 'smiling Sisyphus' to represent the importance of finding meaning and purpose in our struggles in an often-absurd world. Figure 3.2, Sisyphus and the 5M, highlights the effort required to keep the cycle of change turning and going forward and the stoic disposition required to keep it up.

Think About It

In contrast to the cyclist's image, Figure 3.2 highlights the uphill struggle required to keep the change wheel – drawn as a boulder – moving forward. It showcases the smiling determination of the perspiring change agent, who possesses the mindful awareness and mobilized energy necessary to tackle the challenging slope.

How might you contrast the cycle and cyclist in Figure 3.1 and Sisyphus and the boulder in Figure 3.2 to inspire reflection and discussion on the skills, capabilities and disposition of those striving to bring about change? Which dynamic image do you prefer? Can you create one that you find even more compelling?

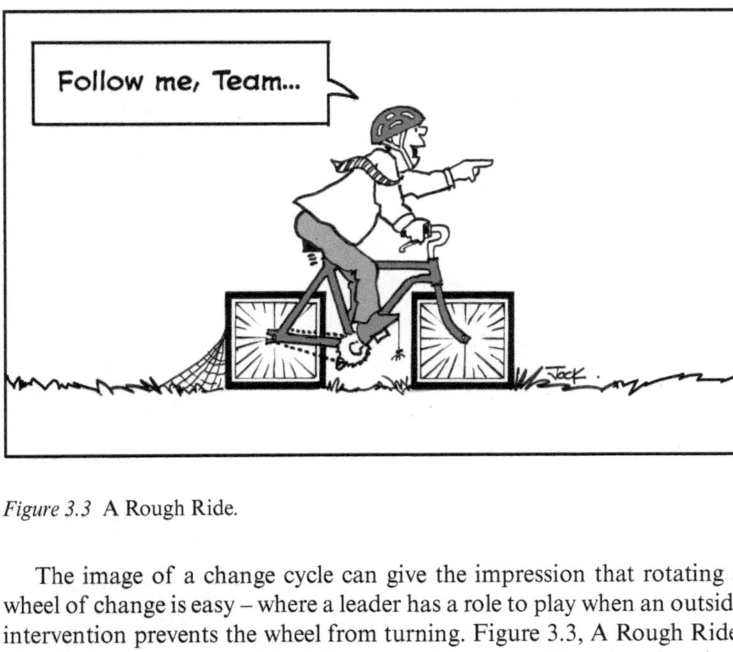

Figure 3.3 A Rough Ride.

The image of a change cycle can give the impression that rotating a wheel of change is easy – where a leader has a role to play when an outside intervention prevents the wheel from turning. Figure 3.3, A Rough Ride, gives a different view and highlights the challenges of keeping the wheel turning. As illustrated in Figure 1.1, conventional change management often thinks within a 'box'. While conventional project management is often a rigid, linear planning sequence, for 5M, it is a creative 'mapping' exercise. While conventional project management often sets formal technical tasks to be executed, for 5M, it is an artful donning of 'masks' in the performance of influence. While conventional project management often advocates a formalized process of monitoring, evaluation and 'ticking off' tasks, 5M highlights the careful construction and selection of 'mirrors' for accurate and useful reflection. Those involved in change often find their attempts to create a productive change cycle frustrated by ineffective thinking 'inside the (traditional) box'. Trying to progress when all you have is square boxes as wheels means aspirational rhetoric ('Follow me team') is out of sync with the realities change agents have to work with.

Think About It

In Figure 3.3, the cyclist confidently points forward, his tie fluttering in the wind, urging his 'team' to follow. However, the wheels, being square boxes, are difficult to turn. The spider, rather cutely hanging off the cyclist's foot, has spun webs that symbolize the inertia caused by the conditions preventing movement and the frequent lack of progress.

How might you use this image to spark discussion and reflection on the inertia created by rigid, 'box-like' thinking in change? Consider the three components of the change wheel. What challenges arise from formal and inflexible planning processes, a technical 'box ticking' approach to planned change tasks, and bureaucratic monitoring and review?

Figure 3.4 Little Boxes, Little Boxes...

Box-like thinking extends from traditional 'Plan-Do-Check' cycles to how organizations divide their labour and manage hierarchies. Formal organization charts often portray people as cogs in a machine or functionaries put into boxes separated from others horizontally and vertically. The result is often slow, bureaucratic, inefficient processes, mind-numbing boredom and frustrated initiative. In addition, the boxes become territories, and decision-making is a fight between competing specialist tribes. As satirized in the classic song, we are placed into, become accustomed to and learn to live within and not challenge our 'Little Boxes'.

Think About It

The image of the innovator and change agent is often portrayed in a positive light, emphasizing qualities like entrepreneurship and even heroism. However, as depicted in Figure 3.4, the reality of organizational life can be quite different. Internal politics and bureaucratic sludge can turn dreams into nightmares, promising careers into disappointments, and win-win outcomes into stressful and frustrating losses and disappointments. This situation can be extremely discouraging for those eager to implement change that transcends boundaries. Yet, it is an unavoidable aspect of organizational life that must be accepted and navigated. As the 5M framework outlines, leading change requires being mindful of these barriers and challenges and working in and around the hierarchy to mobilize energy and support to overcome these obstacles.

To stimulate discussion and reflection on how traditional silos and hierarchies can hinder change initiatives, consider using Figure 3.4, Little Boxes, Little Boxes. Discuss the personal frustrations and career challenges these barriers may present for those initiating change. Cultivating the mindset required to handle such challenges with resilience and determination and developing the skills necessary to address them is essential.

Chapter 3 Self-Test

Select the <u>two best answers</u> **that complete the statements below**. There are several 'half-truths' in the other options to choose from. These capture something important but are misleading if taken too far. The 'correct answers' are in Appendix 1. If your answer is incorrect, you might reflect on how it may be 'half-right' but 'half-wrong'.

1. **Managing change**
   - A. is an expert discipline and the province of specialized change experts.
   - B. controls change initiatives by prescribing actions, creating checklists and monitoring progress.
   - C. is the discipline of influencing ourselves and others to achieve a purpose.
   - D. may be a misleading term in preparing us for tackling the often messy and unpredictable nature of change.

2. **The 5M Framework**

    A. prescribes in detail how to act to bring about change.
    B. is a framework for action. It identifies key issues and strategies for addressing them.
    C. is an expert tool that uses the latest scientific knowledge about best practice change management.
    D. provides advice on how to prepare for, conduct and adjust change initiatives to improve the chances of success.

3. **The perspective on change and its leadership provided by the 5M Framework is**

    A. a frustrating and thankless uphill battle.
    B. an ongoing skilful balancing act.
    C. an easy ride once one has become an expert cyclist.
    D. a challenging enterprise that requires resilience and a sense of humour.

4. **The change cycle is**

    A. a fixed set of tasks in an objective project management process of planning, doing and evaluating change.
    B. an iterative cultural process of mapping the change journey, donning masks to influence others effectively, and deploying mirrors to capture and adapt to the change's progress.
    C. requires a skilled and energetic cyclist to remain balanced while continuing to move forward.
    D. a rigid sequence of events that inevitably occur, whatever the circumstances.

5. **The leader of change or change 'cyclist' is**

    A. on top of everything and in control.
    B. is required to fully consider the political and cultural dimensions of change, as well as its structural and technical features.
    C. mobilizes energy for change and is mindful of barriers and complexity.
    D. someone who directs the energy of others.

6. **The M's in the 5M Framework are designed to capture**

    A. the flexible and iterative Mapping of change and the Masks we adopt to influence others.
    B. 'one best way' of Managing change.
    C. the distorted nature of Mirrors.
    D. the importance of keeping the change cycle going by Mobilizing energy and being Mindful of challenges.

Section 1

Key Takeaways and Resources

Key Takeaways

Chapter 1. The Change Problem

1. **Think outside the box**. Use checklists but address uncertainty, emotion and politics when applying them.
2. **Be careful**. Be mindful of the limited success of conventional change methods and initiatives.
3. **Be realistic**. Uncover, accept and work with and on the biases against and barriers to achieving change.
4. **Bring people along**. Work *with* people's wants and needs. Begin from where they are and energize the pull for change.

Chapter 2. Reimagining Change, Reinventing Yourself

1. **Embrace Janus**. Be ready to work with (and present) a formal front-stage strategic-rational face and an informal backstage messy-emotive face of change.
2. **Flip the iceberg**. Appreciate the importance of the formal technical rational dimension of change (the surface 'tip'). Counter-balance the under-appreciation of its informal, emotional-political and messy nature (the 'bulk') by highlighting the significance of the bulk below the surface.
3. **Ride the rollercoaster**. Expect, appreciate, enjoy and prepare for the journey of ease and difficulty, highs and lows, wins and losses, rapid acceleration and slow, mind-numbing slog.
4. **Be mindful and mobilize**. Be mindful of our unproductive default responses to confronting the realities of change and mobilize yourself and others to acknowledge and overcome them.

DOI: 10.4324/9781032629971-5

Chapter 3. The 5M Framework

- **Managing change is a human capability**. It is a general skill, not a specialized occupation. It is being willing and able to influence ourselves and others effectively.
- **Create a productive change cycle**. Successful change is achieved through a productive cycle of planning, doing and checking. Approaching this cycle by creating Maps, donning Masks and using Mirrors helps capture the uncertainty, emotion and politics of change.
- **Lead by supporting a productive change cycle**. This requires being Mindful of complexity and barriers and Mobilizing energy and support to overcome challenges.
- **Work with yet go beyond silos and hierarchies**. The 5M framework is a guide to achieving success by going beyond conventional change management and working across the lines and between the spaces in the organization chart.

Resources

- *Reimagining Change Website* (www.reimaginingchange.com)
  Introductory video on the homepage.
- *Ironies of Organizational Change*
  'An Invitation' pp. 1–5 Act 1 Reimagining Change
  Ch. 1 'The Change Problem' & Ch. 2 'Reimagining Change, Reinventing Yourself', pp. 21–73.
- *Coursera Program*
  Chapters 1 and 2: Reimagining Change 1: The Change Problem & Reimagining Change 2: Icebergs and Death Valleys
  Nine short video lectures, four readings and four tests.
- *Short Change: An Introduction to Managing Change*
  'Introduction', Ch. 1 'The Discipline of Change' & Ch. 2 'The 5M Framework'.

Section 2

Cycle of Change

4 Mapping Change

Mapping change is the first stage in a *Change Cycle* that includes *Mapping* the journey (orientation), using the appropriate *Masks* (progress through successful performances) and using *Mirrors* (to check on progress and adapt along the way).

Change is often uncertain, and planning for an unpredictable journey is challenging. We use the term mapping to capture this dilemma, highlighting it and providing an ongoing reminder of the challenge it creates. A creative view of 'mapping' a journey is a far better guide than images of 'planning' a route march.

Despite never being an accurate representation, maps provide orientation, confidence and guidance. The intelligent use of maps and mapping techniques provides a basis for action. It also allows reflection and discussion of progress and adaptation.

Unlike map reading, a GPS instructs you along the way and instantly re-routes if you make a mistake. An adaptive change GPS is better than a fixed route map. However, there is a degree of informed scepticism about over-reliance on GPS. When it lures the user into a false sense of certainty, it can lead to ignoring local, existing or changing real-world conditions and lead to disaster if followed unthinkingly. Figure 4.1, A Change GPS captures the irony of a GPS providing hopeless expert advice. It overlays the two popular images of a GPS as an informed, flexible tool and a flawed automated expert. This helps to capture our background awareness of the uncertainty and unpredictability of a change journey that constantly threatens to undermine the 'best-laid plans of mice and men'.

Figure 4.1, also shows the map reader or GPS user standing on an artificial paper map. This alludes to two famous fictional stories about our real-world use and illusory reliance on map accuracy.

The first is a poem by Miroslav Holub that was taken up and popularized in organization studies by Karl Weick (1995, p. 54). It tells the story of a Hungarian lieutenant leading a small detachment in the Alps when it

DOI: 10.4324/9781032629971-7

Figure 4.1 A Change GPS.

began to snow, and they got horribly lost. Then he found a map in his pocket. This calmed them down. They pitched camp and, after the snowstorm, used the map to find their way back to their unit. There was only one problem! When they returned, they found it was a map of the Pyrenees, not the Alps! The moral of the story? It is not just that 'any old map will do', but that reassuring guidance can increase confidence and help people find their way!

The second is a story by Jorge Borges (1999), 'On Exactitude in Science'. It recounts how the Cartography Guild in an Empire, in the search for an accurate map, created a 1:1 scale map of the Empire. The only problem was that it covered the whole country with a paper map that was soon reduced to tatters. The lesson here? All maps are inaccurate, partial representations of the real world. This is why they are helpful but also simplified and potentially misleading.

Think About It

The Polish-born philosopher and scientist Alfred Korzybski (1933) famously stated, 'The map is not the territory'. Yet, if you ponder that thought, you may notice how often we make the mistake of confusing the two. Reflect on Figure 4.1 and consider whether you have observed yourself or others taking our own ideas about the conditions to be faced and what they think should be done for what is real and desirable. Have you noticed yourself or others sticking doggedly to what you think to be real and required and not be ready to question? How well did this work?

How might you use Figure 4.1, A Change GPS, to inspire discussion and reflection on the challenges of changing direction in change? A GPS quickly reroutes after you make a mistake or conditions change. Were you initially or subsequently surprised by the lack of emotion in the automated voice? What does such a response say about the challenges of getting yourself or others to alter a plan? There is humour in the GPS telling the user that he is 'now lost'. What attitude does this reflect on our use of maps and GPSs? Using this image, how might we best develop, adjust and use 'plans' or 'maps' during change?

Figure 4.2 Gap Analysis.

If you want to get from 'A' to 'B', there is always a gap you have to cross. It is one thing to imagine where you want to go. It is another to get there. We often underestimate or even forget this transition challenge.

Figure 4.2, Gap Analysis, reminds us of this. It refers to the now iconic instruction first painted on the platforms of the London Underground: 'Mind the gap' (between the train and the platform). Hundreds, if not thousands, of people are injured by tripping on or falling down this gap every year!

As a mapping technique, gap analysis is a standard management tool. It is simple yet often misused. It involves determining where you are ('As Is') and deciding 'where you want to go ('To Be'). Many users include a third element: 'How to Get There'.

What is the first thing we want to know if you are lost? Where we are going, or where we are? In a sense, this is a conundrum. Knowing where you want to go is important in helping you define where you are while knowing where you are is important in helping you define where you want to go. The change, to repeat, is not the destination but the journey you have to make from where you are to where you want to go.

But what if 'where we are' and 'where we are going' are shifting and unclear? What if the gap is threatening and the uncertainty scary? How do we deal with those who are fearful or dismissive of this uncertainty, who wish to 'Just Do It' and leap thoughtlessly into 'How To' questions?

Think About It

The character in Figure 4.2 is embarking on this 'Analysis'. As we have stressed, change is not the destination but the transition we live through to get there. The cartoon shows the importance and potential anxiety of fully looking into the 'chasm' and working out the 'actual gap'. Notice the sweat coming off her brow as she confronts the task.

How might you use Figure 4.2, Gap Analysis, to foster discussion and reflection on shifting people's focus to understanding change as a 'gap' rather than a destination? Additionally, how can we manage the stress caused by the risks and uncertainties of this gap? Given these challenges, how might you and others effectively create and use a gap analysis?

Figure 4.3 Forcefield Analysis.

Knowing the conditions along the way is important when embarking on a journey. Without this understanding, we do not know how challenging it will be or how to prepare for it.

Forcefield analysis is a standard managing change technique for assessing these conditions. Cliches about how easy or hard change is abound. However, a forcefield analysis aims to identify the real conditions for a particular proposed change. It lists the number and strength of forces for and against the change. One of the traditional insights of change management has been identifying the forces against the change and working out how to remove them. Figure 4.3 Forcefield Analysis, provides a sobering view of these resistant forces. Note how the forces *for* 'change' are pictured, the lonely figure below left, and the forces *against* change that 'preserve' the status quo, the heavily armed equipment and troops on the upper right.

Think About It

After an initial analysis of the need to change and even excitement at the prospect, the journey can often feel lonely and frustrating. It may seem as though everything and everyone is working against you, making it difficult to achieve what you want and what is needed. It's no surprise that one of the most popular topics and critical concerns is 'resistance to change'. Figure 4.3 illustrates how this journey may feel like an uphill battle for the change agent, with little support for change and a powerful and heavily fortified opposition.

How might you use Figure 4.3, Forcefield Analysis, to inspire discussion and reflection on the conditions likely to be encountered on the change journey, as well as the nature and strength of forces for and against change? How might you use it to stimulate conversation about how a realistic acknowledgement of the challenges might appear negative and be demotivating? What strategies might you develop to counteract this perception?

A B

Figure 4.4 Moving Forward (A) and (B).

Once we know where we are, where we are going, and the conditions along the way, we can plan the route! It sounds simple, but there are a number of methods, consultancies and organizations that prescribe a staged checklist route without such considerations. Drawing up a considered plan can be viewed as creating a route map for the change journey.

Figure 4.4A (left) shows a bewildered manager using a standard route map. Note the reference to common steps of the initial 'unfreezing' of the status quo stage, for example create urgency, build a coalition and develop a vision and strategy. The figure captures the sweat, confusion, changes of mind and direction from grappling with the devil in the details as change progresses. The compass may tell us the general direction we have to take, but where do we start? Where should we focus our time and effort? The map is inevitably vague, and must we really do everything in a fixed order? How do we change direction, go back, or explore another route when facing challenges?

In contrast, Figure 4.4B (right) may inspire some hope and optimism. The 'followers' are still lost and confused, surrounded and blinkered by a maze of barriers and consulting their GPS, maps and charts. In this case, the leader uses a ladder to gain a helicopter view of twists and turns to navigate with the team towards the final destination. The leader is inspired and directed by a clear sighting of where they are and where they need to go ('gap analysis') and an informed view of the terrain to be crossed, the enabling paths and the maze of obstacles to be considered along the way ('forcefield analysis').

Think About It

How might you use Figures 4.4A and B to stimulate reflection and discussion on what are believed to be the main stages of the proposed transition? In what ways might prescriptive details be confusing when faced with the 'devil in the details' of change? What kind of a 'ladder' is a planned route map? How might you best use it?

Chapter 4 Self-Test

Select the <u>two best answers that complete</u> the statements below. There are several 'half-truths' in the other options to choose from. These capture something important but are misleading if taken too far. The 'correct answers' are in Appendix 1. If your answer is incorrect, you might reflect on how it may be 'half-right' but 'half-wrong'.

1. **Mapping change is a valuable description of planning change because it**

   A. lets us know that it is never possible to plan a journey.
   B. helps remind us that the map is not the territory, and maps alone won't get us there.
   C. gives us an accurate and complete description of the route we should take.
   D. allows us to use gap, forcefield and route analysis as flexible and practical guides.

2. **A change GPS is an approach to mapping change that**

   A. recognizes the importance of advice on the route to take and is ready to update and change.
   B. requires a computer to capture the complexities of change.
   C. appreciates the confidence and value of having a 'plan' even if it is based on partial knowledge.
   D. gives you a true picture of how to instantly and effectively adapt to changing conditions.

3. **The idea of a change gap and the use of gap analysis**

   A. focuses on two key questions: 'Where are we now?' and 'Where do we want to go?'
   B. includes the cultural, political, structural and technical dimensions of change.
   C. focuses on the end goal without being distracted by the problems of getting there.
   D. is an infallible way to map out the 'real change'.

4. **The change forcefield and the use of forcefield analysis**

   A. focuses on the forces resisting change.
   B. provides a vehicle for discussing the real forces that must be considered in change.
   C. captures the terrain that must be considered in planning the route to take.
   D. provides an objective account of the likelihood of change success or failure.

5. **The route analysis**

   A. charts the progress through the stages of change and is adapted to the conditions identified in the Gap and the Force Field analyses.
   B. shows how Lewin's three stages of 'unfreezing', 'moving' and 're-freezing' are irrelevant and misleading.
   C. rigidly sticks to a planned sequence of stages.
   D. uses the 'Gap' and 'Force Field' analyses to determine which issues are the most significant and when and how they should be addressed.

6. **The map is not the territory means**

   A. all maps are useless, and one should give up on creating or using them.
   B. maps are comprehensive and accurate views of the terrain and how to traverse it.
   C. we should not be fooled into thinking we have found 'the' plan for change.
   D. we should be continually aware of the partial nature of our knowledge and the need to revise when necessary.

5 Masks of Change

Knowing what to do to manage change is one thing. Knowing how to do it is another. While the route map outlines what you must do, you must decide how to do it in context and with others. How change plans are executed is always a performance, the artful exercise of influence in time, space and conditions that are often not of our choosing. In this chapter, you will discover the performances you will have to give, the masks you will need to wear, the tensions and dilemmas you will encounter and why influencing yourself is central to your ability to influence others.

Figure 5.1 Juggling Masks.

DOI: 10.4324/9781032629971-8

Masks were at the heart of any transformation on a Greco-Roman stage. The exercise of influence in bringing about change is a series of performances in which we put on various masks and play many parts.

Mapping change provides us with scripts to follow. These scripts then have to be enacted, and performances are given on stage, in the moment, in front of audiences to achieve the desired effect. In an important sense, the tasks outlined as a sequence of actions on a change journey are a series of more or less influential performances that mobilize and persuade people to make the transition happen. We use the term masks to emphasize this fact and highlight the different roles change leaders have to play to influence multiple stakeholders or audiences effectively.

The conventional mask of the Manager is that of the rational controller. It involves traditional 'command and control' tasks such as planning and budgeting, organizing, staffing, controlling and problem-solving.

As a Leader, however, the focus is on winning hearts and minds, mobilizing energy and motivation. It consists of establishing direction, aligning people, motivating, inspiring and ultimately producing sustainable change.

Both roles are important yet require different skills and performances. The change agent, as a systematic, responsible project Manager, is a cool, rational and detail-oriented character who specifies, monitors and holds everyone to task. The change Leader is a more emotive and energizing figure. (S)he is less concerned with details and controls and more with creating visions, establishing a sense of meaningful purpose and energizing and inspiring people to bring these about.

We also don multiple masks when playing out these roles. Influencing *events* involves playing the parts of both a Planner and an Improviser. Influencing *people* involves juggling the roles of an engaging Participative leader and a forceful Directive one. These are multidimensional performances, and there is no simple one-best-way solution.

Many of us, however, have preferences and capabilities that align more with one another. And when we are required to think and act in different ways, we often find the dilemmas challenging and appear to be 'two-faced' uncomfortable. However, donning different masks is not about being deceitful or inauthentic. The most persuasive performances draw on personality features we possess. It is about controlling rather than being controlled by the masks we wear.

Think About It

Do you find yourself playing the Manager or Leader role at work or in your private life? Do you find one or the other easier and preferable to play? How well do you handle yourself, and how might you improve your ability to perform the less comfortable role?

How might you use Figure 5.1, Juggling Masks, to inspire discussion and reflection on the masks we wear in change, the need for yet limitations of each and how you might address the stresses and challenges of 'juggling'? How many masks have you worn in previous attempts to influence others and bring about a recent change in yourself, in your personal life, or at work? How did this go?

Figure 5.2 The Promethean Challenge.

In ancient Greek mythology, Prometheus was the Titan who defied Zeus by stealing fire and giving it to humanity, thus enabling progress and civilization. In this enterprise, Prometheus symbolized Western faith in science, rationality and the ability to control nature (and, in our case, change) for our ends. He did so at a cost, however. Zeus punished the immortal Prometheus for his theft by chaining him to a rock for all eternity. Each day, an eagle ate his liver, only to have it grow back overnight, so the eagle feasted again the following day. His fate symbolized humanity's hubris, an overconfidence in our knowledge and ability to control nature (and, in our case, change), often with disastrous results. The power of the myth lies in the tension it captures.

Is our pursuit of and confidence in knowledge and techniques for managing change a positive force for progress, or an illusion and a curse with dangerous outcomes and unpredictable consequences? It raises key change management questions:

1. How far should one attempt to control and regulate people and events?
2. How much should one plan and stick to it, and how much should one expect the unexpected and be willing and able to improvise?
3. Are there limits beyond which it's immoral, unsustainable or self-defeating to tread in our quest to control change?

How can we best act to control events with limited knowledge and live in an uncertain world? What masks do we have to wear, what roles do we have to play, what tasks do we have to undertake and what performances do we have to give? What capabilities do we need to have, and what behaviours do we have to excel at? Different and opposing views of what is required exist, and we characterize the challenge of grappling with them as the Promethean Challenge.

On the one hand, we have an image of Planned Change. In such a view, change occurs through a relatively predictable set of stages. As a **Planner**, the change agent with foresight and control can be Directive. They use the knowledge and techniques we possess to manage change effectively.

On the other hand, we view change as an uncertain, complex and emergent process. In this case, the change agent is more akin to an **Improviser**, adapting to, minimizing the costs of and using whatever opportunities arise from inherently unpredictable events. The image is more of a Navigator than a Planner. It involves using charts, sails and a rudder to steer a course in the face of wind and tides out of our control.

Think About It

Do you feel more comfortable approaching change as a **Planner**, using a rule book, setting specific goals, and creating defined schedules? Or do you prefer to be an **Improviser**, establishing a rough direction, being open to the unexpected, and adapting rapidly to changing conditions?

What skills and temperament do you think each mask and performance requires, and how might you further develop these qualities in yourself? Consider how you can best prepare to create and follow plans when they are feasible and desirable while also skilfully navigating turbulent and changing conditions, improvising and adapting to the unexpected. Reflect on your change management style and how it aligns with these two approaches.

Think of Figure 5.2, a fit and strong Prometheus chained to a rock, who we know is condemned to a life of pain. How can this image stimulate discussion and reflection on the value and yet dangers of our faith in our knowledge and the plans we make? Note the neutral expression – neither happy confidence nor painful despair. How should we feel about our planning?

Figure 5.3 The Machiavellian Challenge.

In organizations and societies where people are diverse in character, fickle and changeable in their wants and behaviours, how do we best act to influence and control them (to bring about desired change)? To exercise such influence, what tasks do we have to undertake and what roles do we have to play? As a behavioural challenge, what masks do we have to wear, and what performances are we required to give on-stage at the moment? As with controlling events, there are different opposing views about how best to influence and control people. For the following reasons, we describe the challenges this presents as the Machiavellian Challenge.

In 1514, Machiavelli (2005) wrote *The Prince*, his infamous handbook for how princes must behave to acquire or retain power. In contrast to the humanistic and religious guidelines and principles of the time, Machiavelli promised to 'tell it how it is', 'warts and all', offering realistic advice based on how people are rather than how we might like them to be. Yet he did so at a cost, calling the game is a dangerous activity. In the popular mind, Machiavelli has been demonized for recommending manipulation, fear and deceit in political affairs. His work was even initially banned by the Pope. Since then, Machiavelli has become a symbol of the use of 'black arts'.

Recently, however, that view has been challenged. Machiavelli has been praised for his 'brutal honesty' and the pragmatic advice he offers to those grappling with the realities of power. Now, Machiavelli is celebrated for calling the game. Something is appealing about his exposing the hypocrisy of leaders who pretend to be principled and act for the greater good yet, behind the scenes, act in their self-interest, indulging in manipulation, coercion and deceit. Machiavelli is renowned for opening up this issue of what is termed *realpolitik*. How do those in power *actually* behave, and how do they have to behave? He is also renowned for posing the central question regarding this behaviour: whether it is better to be loved than feared, or the contrary. The answer is that one would like to be both one and the other. But since it is challenging to be both together, it is much safer to be feared than loved when one of the two must be lacking.

The importance of 'winning hearts and minds' is commonly accepted in influencing people to change in desirable ways. Yet, what's more debatable is what's required to achieve this.

Following Machiavelli:

> What is better? To inspire through hope or create fear? A charismatic appeal or a dictator's threat? Are people ultimately motivated by running to what they idealize and aspire to? Or running from what they're scared about and threatened by?

Think About It

We prefer to believe the former. But is this what we would like to think, or what is indeed the case? When you feverishly get an assignment or proposal in at the last minute, is this inspiration or fear of missing the deadline? When people are consulted and called upon in public, are they inspired by their ideals or fearful of being shamed? Does the phrase, 'If you can't change the people, change the people!' resonate with some of the frustration we feel when facing what we perceive to be counter-productive behaviour and irrational resistance? Is 'fight or flight' a more familiar, desirable or undesirable response to threatening conflict, compromise and collaboration?

Do you prefer being a more Participative or Coercive leader, encouraging involvement and stimulating inspiration and hope or being forcefully directive using dictate, fear and threat to overcome apathy and opposition? How might you choose or blend such strategies? How might you develop your capabilities and create more compelling performances in either area, particularly when it involves donning a mask and acting in ways you are uncomfortable with?

How might you use Figure 5.3, The Machiavellian Challenge, to inspire reflection and discussion on handling the stigma attached to any admissions that using fear and coercion is part of change and sometimes required? Foster discussion on how far you and others feel that 'Machiavellian' strategies are evil and always counter-productive or a relieving and useful brutal honesty about what it really takes.

Figure 5.4 Public and Backstage Performances.

The exercise of influence on people and events as a Planner, Improviser, Participative or Directive leader requires performances on two stages: formally, upfront and in public, and informally, behind the scenes and in private. These two performances often clash. Successful change professionals are willing and able to creatively separate or blend these performances to fit different audiences and conditions.

Although the meaning of Figure 5.4 is not immediately obvious, it has several layers and is possibly our favourite. Marc Anthony's famous funeral oration for Julius Caesar highlights the importance of leaders influencing people through the artful balancing of public 'frontstage' and private 'backstage' performances. A key to leading change is juggling multiple audiences, levels of meaning and agendas and aligning them to motivate and create support is key to leading change.

In this famous speech from Shakespeare's (1999) [1599] play, Julius Caesar's friend Marc Anthony appears to be praising Caesar's murderer, Brutus, while simultaneously undermining the credibility of Brutus and his allies and garnering support for Caesar. This artful performance is appreciated by Caesar's supporters as well. As the Roman soldiers note 'backstage', Marc Anthony says he comes to 'Bury Caesar', but his speech is all about undermining and 'burying' Brutus.

The message here is not that one must lie in public or that leaders must be ironic to give persuasive speeches. Figure 5.4 points out that leaders face frontstage expectations and backstage commentaries. To be successful, they must attend to both. Sometimes, this may be saying one thing in public and another in private. Still, at other times, it means juggling multiple meanings in giving persuasive frontstage performances while simultaneously capturing and addressing backstage criticisms and commentaries.

The storylines we have to work with are well-established. Change programmes are presented as rational and efficient enterprises. This view is represented in official policies and procedures, statements to customers and the public, as well as written up and verbalized in meetings, agendas and minutes. The sociologist Erving Goffman described it as the 'frontstage' public performance of organizational life. It is the view we present, and like to present, to stakeholders and ourselves about rationality and efficiency. As managers, we have to make a formal case for change, create legitimacy and build confidence by acting and talking with certainty about our plans and the outcomes these will generate. As leaders, we motivate through unifying and inspirational visions of a common and higher purpose. We ignore all such activities at our peril.

Change issues also involve what Goffman (2022 [1959]) described as 'backstage'. In this realm, we find a different language spoken. It's what some decision-making experts have described as the '*rhetoric of realpolitik*'. It's a world of commentary upon formal organizational performance, a realm in which tales of confusion, intrigue, incompetence, vested interest and even chaos are told. It's what is talked about in bars, over the water cooler and during the coffee breaks in ritualized meetings. Backstage performances involve all the pragmatic, emotional and political behind-the-scenes work needed to prop up the change initiative. To win over 'hearts and minds', change managers and leaders must be able to acknowledge such realities and reveal themselves as a person behind the mask, a 'beating heart' behind the 'stuffed shirt'. Such backstage performances may seem more real and off-the-cuff than actions on the formal stage, but they make their own demands on how we need to appear. Reviews of evidence for management competencies in bringing about change emphasize both strategic and visionary frontstage capabilities and interpersonal and political backstage skills.

Think About It

As Stanford Professor Jeffrey Pfeffer put it, the 'skills of getting things done' are just as important as the 'skills of figuring out what to do'. Following the change maps we have created is a travelling art; enacting the change scripts we have created requires a virtuoso performance. An effective performance is far from automatic. It requires professional rehearsal, rhetorical dexterity, interpersonal skilfulness, emotional intelligence and self-control.

This chapter has introduced you to some key masks you must put on and take off, juggle or blend. Consider now how you might successfully play the role of the Manager or Leader, Planner or Improviser, Participative or Directive change champion *both frontstage and backstage*. In what ways are these similar or different, overlapping or in conflict? How do you feel personally about this juggling process? Does it feel inauthentic or exciting, stressful or energizing? As we will explore further in the next chapter, how might you take time out to assess how you are doing and work on improving?

How might you use Figure 5.4 to stimulate reflection and discussion on how to effectively address both frontstage and backstage audiences without appearing two-faced or inauthentic? Who are the 'Brutuses' and the 'soldiers' in any change you observe or embark upon? How do you motivate people by acknowledging and incorporating the celebratory body language and upbeat demeanour of Marc Anthony and the worried and concerned look of the soldiers?

Chapter 5 Self-Test

Select the two best answers **that complete the statements below**. There are several 'half-truths' in the other options to choose from. These capture something important but are misleading if taken too far. The 'correct answers' are in Appendix 1. If your answer is incorrect, you might reflect on how it may be 'half-right' but 'half-wrong'.

1. **Juggling multiple masks**

   A. is a key part of the different change roles we have to play.
   B. has to be done effectively to give persuasive performances.
   C. is a source of tension and inauthenticity that must be avoided at all costs.
   D. is easy; we don't have to work at it; we just have to be ourselves.

2. **Implementing change involves**

   A. effectively influencing people.
   B. identifying tasks to be done and providing detailed instructions on what to do.
   C. tailoring how you (ex)press yourself to what will (im)press others.
   D. being manipulative and deceitful in masking your real self.

3. **The masks of the Manager and the Leader are**

   A. incompatible and impossible for one person to juggle or combine.
   B. both important in creating effective performances that motivate and drive others.

C. are how we enact complementary roles in controlling people and events.
D. no longer relevant. Change agents must be leaders, first and foremost.

4. **The Promethean challenge involves**

A. giving up on trying to control events, avoiding the pain and suffering inflicted on us by people and misfortune.
B. informed and intelligent planning so we do not incur the costs of rectifying mistakes.
C. creatively blending flexible planning and responsible improvisation.
D. planning where we can and being adaptive when we cannot.

5. **The Machiavellian challenge involves**

A. adjusting how forceful or participative one is depending on people and circumstances.
B. creatively blending the use of fear and hope to motivate people to change.
C. using fear and deceit to ensure people follow the path you prescribe.
D. giving up on being honest with others or allowing them to be really involved.

6. **To 'win hearts and minds' we need to**

A. be hypocrites, always being one person in public and another in private.
B. be prepared to appear certain and authoritative, particularly in public, and, often behind the scenes, acknowledge uncertainty and fallibility.
C. show that in reality, our public performances are fake.
D. give public and private performances that are, at times, different and, at other times, creatively blend separate messages to different audiences.

6 Mirrors of Change

Leaders of change initiatives are faced with known unknowns but also *unknown unknowns*. Uncertainty is endemic, complexity is unavoidable and denial is widespread. How do you evaluate your progress and adjust your course before it is too late in such contexts? How do you create early warning signals? In this chapter, you will discover the value of experimentation and evaluation, examine and critically analyse methods for monitoring intellectual, emotional and practical capabilities and progress (the head, hand and heart) and learn how to create effective and practical learning spaces within change initiatives.

Figure 6.1 Mirror, Mirror on the Wall.

Many of us have a love/hate relationship with mirrors. Sometimes, we want the truth, yet at other times, we don't. We sometimes deny what we see in mirrors but still can't resist looking into them. We might even have

DOI: 10.4324/9781032629971-9

that favourite mirror in the house. We want to see a flattering image that reaffirms a 'preferred' picture of ourselves and our activities. Remember Snow White's evil stepmother's, '*Mirror, mirror, on the wall, who is the fairest of them all?*' We are particularly sensitive to those mirrors that tell us what we are like and how others see and judge us.

In a sense, we all have a 'looking-glass self' that is very much concerned with keeping up appearances. In checking up on how we look and deciding how we should act, we use multiple mirrors in different ways. For example, we use both side-view and rear-view car mirrors to capture what is beside and behind us to help us act appropriately when looking forward. But remember the warning on car side mirrors: 'Objects in the mirror are closer than they appear'! Coming to terms with using a hall of mirrors requires a playful appreciation of how partial and distorted mirrors can be.

The metaphor of 'mirrors' captures the all-too-human, often partial and even distorted nature of the means we use to reflect on who we are and how we are going.

In the managerial 'plan–do–check' view of a change cycle, the 'check' is a rational technical step of monitoring and evaluating. It confirms if tasks are done and checks how well they are completed. This process has a role. Surgeons, pilots and engineers raising skyscrapers all use checklists. It rarely ends well when they don't. Managing change also requires checklists. But the 'mirror' image highlights that just ticking the boxes is not enough.

The leadership 'maps-masks-mirrors' cycle reminds us that change and its evaluation are symbolic and meaning-laden transition processes. To accurately capture how change is going, we must seriously address all the psychological, cultural and political issues and agendas that can distort how 'we' see 'ourselves.

Firstly, how we see ourselves is influenced by the 'voices in our heads' that we have inherited from significant others in the past. The interpretation of what we 'see' is never simply 'our own'; it is sensible to be mindful of this.

Secondly, reflections on a change programme are never just about us. It also involves the perceptions and interests of all those driving or affected by the change. The 'reflection' we seek goes beyond us to include the views of all those important to the change process. The woman, as a change agent, is looking into a mirror that includes multiple views of herself and what she is involved in.

As we navigate the change terrain, our actions are influenced by our assumptions about what other people think and feel and what they are up to. Moreover, as every action is, in a sense, an experiment, we require timely and accurate feedback on how things are going so we can adjust to unforeseen outcomes and events. Hence, monitoring and evaluating progress and being aware of the partiality and bias of the mirrors we deploy are essential.

Think About It

List out what evaluation methods you might use to monitor progress in a change. Using the mirror metaphor, in what ways are these likely to be partial, distorted and their accuracy affected by the perceptions and interests of ourselves and others? How might you allow for these limitations and create a valuable hall of mirrors?

In Figure 6.1, Mirror, Mirror on the Wall, the woman is washing her hands and checking on her reflection with an expression that is neither a smile nor a frown. She can see her reflection but also that of a 'ghostly' crowd.

How might you use this cartoon to stimulate reflection and discussion on how far we use mirrors to get an accurate or flattering image of ourselves and the influence of others on what we see and how we judge?

Figure 6.2 Agile Learning.

When someone tells you, '*Make time for reflection and learning*', you most probably want to scream, '*WHEN*?!!' But then, you nod your head because you know you should be taking this on board.

In a world of constant change, competitive environments and increased pressure, there seems to be insufficient time and space to reflect and learn. Yet, we need to. As the retired lieutenant general and US Congressman Bergman noted, it is as if '*There is never enough time to do it right, but always enough time to do it over*' (Badham and Santiago, 2023, p. 133). Unfortunately, this is *not* a recipe for success. So, how do we keep our balance and learn to improve continuously while travelling at the speed of change?

As an ongoing cyclical process, change requires us to:

- beware of outdated yet often preferred images of ourselves and our programmes – our often 'favourite' mirror! (variously described as the 'planning fallacy' or 'optimism bias').
- ditch the autopilot and re-assess plans and perspectives – taking time to use the mirror, not denying or distorting what one sees, acting on what we see, and
- take the initiative and keep the train on the tracks (or the plane flying) rather than just observing and waiting for the train wreck or complaining that there is no time or opportunity to repair or change course.

All these activities are placed in real time, using multiple mirrors to capture:

- the effectiveness of action and events at the moment, and repairing or adjusting course where possible (reflection-in-action)
- how things have gone, and how to improve in the future (reflection-on-action), as well as
- evaluating how well our evaluation methods are working (reflection-on-reflection on action.

Think About It

How can we be agile and creative when establishing and using mirrors? By using popular metaphors like the explorer, we have to be comfortable with, even seek out the unknown; like the experimenter, we have to view actions as experiments and be ready to 'fail forward fast' and learn from the experience; and like the jazz musician, we have to attend carefully to changing conditions and what others are doing and be ready to improvise and adapt.

How might you use Figure 6.2, Agile Learning to inspire reflection and discussion on the challenges of learning as we go? Note that three people are mending the engine, wing and skin while the plane is flying, while two others are looking warily around at others while re-painting and climbing. What stresses does this capture? How might you address them? How might you use this cartoon to consider the challenges of 'pivoting' during change? If the pilot must change directions in ways that might be risky and require even more 'repairs', how can this be sold to passengers and crew as beneficial 'agile learning'?

Figure 6.3 Changing Measures.

We need to know what we are looking for to reflect on how we are doing. This is where the importance of measures and measuring comes in. When relevant and used correctly, our measures capture our 'vital signs' and help us 'take our pulse'. If they are not, they only distract and distort. They become a 'Procrustean Bed' – after Procrustes, the bandit from Greek mythology who stretched or amputated travellers' limbs to make them conform to the length of his bed. The danger lies in force-fitting our actions to meet artificial measures. This does not help us to learn and adapt. In 2011, the Economist Intelligence Unit (2011) confirmed that the 'lack of clearly defined and/or achievable milestones and objectives to track progress' is the #1 factor in determining the failure of change initiatives!

Relevant measures are essential for three key reasons: they help us track progress and identify what still needs to be done; they serve as an early warning system that alerts us to potential issues, allowing us to address them proactively; and they motivate us and others, as clear wins boost confidence, reassure stakeholders and provide opportunities for celebration. Measuring involves metrics but transcends them. Effort and discipline are necessary to avoid promoting excessive accuracy and creating an imbalance in what is being considered.

Regarding accuracy, we all tend to seek confirmation of our beliefs, wish to feel that everything is going smoothly, and want to reassure stakeholders that all is well. As a result, both personal and institutional pressures can lead us to be selective in what we examine and communicate. While a certain level of confidence and optimism is beneficial, it must not devolve into denial or repression. Such attitudes can hinder effective responses to problems and obstruct adaptive action.

To address potential imbalances in change initiatives, it is crucial that the measures we use capture the dynamics of change and assess motivation effectively. Specifically, these measures should include three components: They must reflect the individuals' beliefs about the change and its progress (head), should consider feelings about the change and its impact (heart), and assess how capable and effective people feel they are enacting the change (hand). Far too often, change initiatives have a bias towards a technical and static assessment of whether planned tasks have been completed and performance objectives met. While of significant importance, this approach frequently overlooks the significance of individual's beliefs about whether the right things are being done and achieved (are they 'right in the head'), their emotional engagement in the process (is their 'heart' in it), and their confidence in their ability in contributing to the change (how 'handy' are they and their actions). Since 'self-efficacy' is a vital motivator, understanding beliefs and feelings about one's ability to act effectively is essential for a comprehensive evaluation of motivation in change processes.

Think About It

Have you ever noticed that the ways you measure changes don't give you an accurate or useful assessment of your progress? Have you found yourself in situations where the required measures feel artificial and irrelevant? What experiences have you had with effective measures that are valuable and practical? What principles should you consider when selecting relevant measures?

How can Figure 6.3, Changing Measures be used to foster reflection and open discussions about creating relevant measures? The man in the figure perceives what he wants to see rather than the reality of the situation. In contrast, the woman's concerned expression reflects the anxiety and demotivation that arise from realizing that what is being perceived is often more about what people wish to see rather than the truth. What strategies can be employed to address these challenges when developing appropriate measures?

Figure 6.4 Learning Spaces.

Learning during change is not academic. It is a contact sport. It is experiential, uncertain and often upsetting and controversial. Figure 6.4, Learning Spaces illustrates how learning environments often occur in group settings. They can all too easily turn into a 'blame game' and prevent raising potentially embarrassing or controversial issues.

Learning spaces require creating challenging yet safe 'holding environments' as a potentially embarrassing, upsetting and controversial experience. In real-world change initiatives, there are always 'undiscussable' issues, problems and behaviours; often, the fact that these are undiscussable is also undiscussable! Creating learning spaces to raise such issues safely is a crucial yet practically and politically challenging enterprise.

Individuals can be overly protective, and institutions regularly create defensive routines that inhibit the discussion of controversial issues. Common strategies for cover-up include hiding concerns behind 'displays of conformity' and having biases embedded in cultures and structures. These biases 'build in' or promote discussions of acceptable issues and 'build out' or discourage the acknowledgement of unacceptable ones. As a result, people in the organization might act as if they completely agree with the accepted norms or ideas, even if they have reservations or are aware of existing problems. They tend to avoid standing out or challenging the status quo, which makes it harder for issues to be openly addressed.

Organizations often have a built-in preference towards discussing only certain topics and ignoring others, and this bias becomes part of the culture. Therefore, a key component in developing measures for learning is the creation of learning spaces where people can openly, safely and creatively use these measures and develop strategies for addressing the challenges these raise. Achieving this requires time, effort, psychological sensitivity and political acumen – but the rewards make the effort worthwhile!

To effectively support experiential learning, learning spaces need to be practice-based, outcome-oriented and 'up close and personal', situated near the action. Metaphors of the 'practice field' and the 'rehearsal' have been used as guides. Where do sports teams practice? Not 'offsite' but 'on the field'. Sports are often physical, confrontational, interactive and contextual. 'Practical skills' are intellectual, emotional and situational. They are 'up close and personal'. Where do actors rehearse their performances? Not just in scripting studios but 'on stage'. Viewing learning as rehearsal highlights interaction with others as a key part of preparation and practice, creating a safe environment to receive feedback, embracing mistakes and testing improvements and learning from acting out in situ. To apply these principles to change initiatives implies that our learning should take place close to the action, for example, 'timeouts' in a meeting, reflection at the end, and involve experiments and testing in real life, real-time and real contexts, for example, in a 'pilot site', trialling experimental ideas.

Think About It

Have you noticed that while you and others are committed to learning and improvement, putting these ideas into practice is often challenging? Is the learning too abstract or difficult to apply? Do you find yourself and others avoiding uncomfortable topics or difficult changes? Have there been instances where these challenges were overcome, leading to genuine improvement? If so, what factors contributed to that success? How would you promote and encourage such conditions in a change initiative?

How might you use Figure 6.4, Learning Spaces to encourage reflection and discussion on avoiding the tendency in learning to devolve into a 'blame game'? Pay attention to the goat's dejected expression, the colleague next to him who is turning away and the worried disapproval of the other colleague.

How can we create space to focus on real problems instead of limiting ourselves to 'acceptable' issues?

Chapter 6 Self-Test

Select the <u>one best answer</u> that completes the statements below. There are several 'half-truths' in the other options to choose from. These capture something important but are misleading if taken too far. The 'correct answers' are in Appendix 1. If your answer is incorrect, you might reflect on how it may be 'half-right' but 'half-wrong'.

1. **The use of 'mirrors' as a metaphor for reflection and learning**

   A. emphasizes the importance of accurate reflection.
   B. highlights the significance we attach to visual images.
   C. means avoiding the use of quantitative assessments and financial measures.
   D. captures our common sense understanding of the distortions our biases create.

2. **Ongoing review and evaluation in change involves**

   A. creatively blending multiple touch points, mindful of the partiality and limitations of each.
   B. avoiding discussions about problems and challenges to maintain confidence and build momentum.
   C. simply identifying key performance measures and developing useable quantitative indicators for them.
   D. using qualitative measures to capture the dominant change narrative.

3. **Agile learning in change initiatives is**

   A. ensuring relevant and extensive upfront planning to speed up implementation.
   B. a linear, step-by-step process that occurs throughout the change.
   C. a dynamic, iterative process of identifying problems, brainstorming and rapidly implementing solutions.
   D. giving permission for open experimentation with different strategies and diverse options.

4. **The purpose of measuring change is to**

   A. identify failures and hold those responsible accountable for their mistakes.
   B. streamline change initiatives by removing redundant activities and personnel.

C. ensure financial accountability.
D. track progress, provide early warnings and capture and increase motivation.

5. **A learning space in organizational change is**

A. a digital platform for online learning.
B. a safe yet challenging environment for surfacing concerns and experimenting with solutions.
C. a high-pressure environment designed to uncover and remove resistance to change.
D. a place to have coffee and take a break from the stresses of change.

6. **Creating learning spaces**

A. overcomes all denial and defensiveness.
B. involves addressing the psychological, cultural and political barriers to learning.
C. means directing attention to the views of others, not ourselves.
D. establishes objective measures and formal review processes.

Section 2

Key Takeaways and Resources

Key Takeaways

Chapter 4. Mapping Change

- **Build and operate a change GPS**. Develop the ability to plan, adjust a plan and handle the tensions this creates.
- **Prepare a gap analysis**. Understand the scope of the change by detailing the distance to be travelled between 'where we are now' and 'where we want to be'.
- **Conduct a force field analysis**. Identify the known conditions and forces to be encountered on the journey, which must be considered when planning the route.
- **Create a route map**. Design a guide for the change journey that charts progress through the stages of change (beginning, middle and end) and adapts the map to the conditions identified in the gap and forcefield analyses.

Chapter 5. Masks of Change

- **Develop the capability to juggle masks**. In order to turn maps into successful journeys be prepared to use different masks to perform effectively and exercise influence.
- **Be ready to be a planner and an improviser**. Learn to appreciate and handle the tensions of blending roles and performances.
- **Be positively Machiavellian**. Adjust strategies of participation and coercion, honesty and deceit, to the situation at hand, and be prepared to give a performance that is not criticized for being negatively 'Machiavellian'.
- **Blend frontstage and backstage performances**. Offer credible displays of certainty while acknowledging fallibility. Support aspirations for change but respond to uncertainties and fears.

DOI: 10.4324/9781032629971-10

Chapter 6. Mirrors of Change

- **Be openly reflective**. Use multiple mirrors for reflection and be mindful of their biases and your own.
- **Learn in real time**. Recognize and address the challenges of creating time and space for learning and pivoting, before, during and after action – under pressure and at speed.
- **Measure the right things**. Establish measures to monitor, alert and motivate during periods of change. These should include strategic objectives and performance outcomes (head), the state of people's feelings and emotions (heart) and practical challenges related to implementation (hand).
- **Create learning spaces**. Focus on the difficulties of creating open and meaningful discussion forums and exploratory practice fields close to the action. Encourage surfacing undiscussables and avoid assigning blame for mistakes.

Resources

- *Ironies of Organizational Change*
  Act 2 The Cycle of Change
  Ch. 4 'Maps and Orientation'; Ch. 5 'Masks and Performance'; and Ch. 6 'Mirrors and Reflection', pp. 74–150.
- *Coursera Program*
  Creating a Change Cycle 1: Maps and Orientation; Creating a Change Cycle 2: Masks and Performance; and Creating a Change Cycle 3: Mirrors and Reflection
  Twelve short video lectures, six readings and six tests.
- *Short Change: An Introduction to Managing Change*
  Ch. 5 'Mapping Change', Ch. 6 'Masks of Change' & Ch. 7 'Mirrors of Change'.
- *Power, Politics and Organizational Change*
  First Edition (1999) Ch. 4 'Men Behaving Badly', Ch. 5 'The Entrepreneurial Hero' and Ch. 6 'The Politics of Failure and the Failure of Politics', pp. 99–1.
  Second Edition (2008) Ch. 4. 'Men Behaving Badly', Ch. 6 'Entrepreneurial Heroes' and Ch. 7 'The Good, the Bad and the Ugly', pp. 115–149, 173–211, 212–245.
  Third Edition (2020) Ch. 5 'Cutting the Bullshit', Ch. 6 'Telling Tales', Ch. 7 'Speaking Up', pp. 155–222.

Section 3

Leading Change

Figure 7.1 The Dip.

'change' as a personal and cultural 'transition' that requires adjustment and adaptation by the change leader. The J-curve identifies the need to address an initial drop in productivity and morale in the face of resistance, confusion or disruption; the more profound sense of frustration and loss at the 'bottom' of the dip; and recovering from the 'dip' and realizing improvements beyond what existed before. It also highlights the contrast between these realities of change and the unrealistic rhetoric that often rationalizes change as a simple upward path to progress.

Being *aware* that such challenges exist is one thing. *Attending* to them with focus and discipline is another. *Accepting* that they exist and meeting them with energy and sympathy is yet another.

Think About It

In Figure 7.1, The Dip, the thought bubble of the paraglider captures how change initiatives are often misrepresented in public and practice – as a linear upward path to a productivity-enhancing and morale-boosting strategic goal. Underestimating the challenges to be overcome, the result is all too often the dangers and disasters illustrated by the cartoon's 'Valley of Death'. Note also the desperate but inadequate attempts by those attempting to recover from the 'crash'!

How often do people and organizations define change as the endpoint, not the nature of the journey to get there? Have you experienced yourself or others going into 'fight or flight' when you meet unexpected resistance, problems, and challenges, i.e. lashing out unproductively or giving up on the endeavour? How do you think senior management responds when you try to explain the challenges and what is required to address them? What might you do to gain their support?

How might you use Figure 7.1 to inspire reflection and discussion on the character and costs of a mindless approach to leading change?

Figure 7.2 Mind the Gap(s).

The principles underlying the change cycle are well recognized but often not implemented. There are frequent gaps between what *needs* to get done, what we know should be done and what resources are available. Figure 7.2, Mind the Gap(s), illustrates that we need to tread with care when what we think is a simple step and solid ground is actually an illusion in our heads!

Change leaders routinely need to be mindful of and confront three main gaps.

The first is a *leadership gap* in organizations, where traditional management approaches are often preferred over contemporary leadership practices. Traditional management tends to be egocentric, creative, self-interested and impulsive, prioritizing predictability and control over motivation and innovation. It severely underestimates the degree of behavioural change needed and the actions necessary to impel people to make these changes. Addressing this gap means letting go of traditional mindsets and securities. Managers often feel more comfortable dealing with the rational 'tip of the iceberg' rather than addressing the emotional or relational aspects involved. As individuals and organizations, we are more practised in handling matters of the head than affairs of the heart.

The second is a *practice gap* between our theoretical knowledge and generic techniques and the know-how required to apply these in practice successfully. In figurative terms, there's a difference between the map and the territory or the menu and the meal. In technical terms, there is a gap between filling out checklists and making things happen or what rules prescribe and what situations demand. The result? No matter how much knowledge you collect or how sophisticated the methods you apply, more is always required. The English philosopher Gilbert Ryle spoke of the fundamental difference between 'knowing that' and 'knowing how'. Knowing we have tools available doesn't add up to 'practical knowledge' or knowing how to apply these tools and make things happen in complex and challenging situations.

The third is the *power gap*, as we are rarely given sufficient time and resources to complete effectively the jobs we are formally allocated. A power gap exists between what managers are expected, requested or required to do and the time, people and resources they're given or have available to get their job done. Successful change often depends on multiple groups with different interests and views, many of which change agents do not control. Achieving change often requires contributions from traditionally powerless or disadvantaged groups who are, understandably, resentful, reluctant and resistant. Those initiating change also frequently over-promise, unaware of what is fully required to deliver. In short, we often lack the power to get things done.

When confronted by each of these gaps, a reflex response is to think and feel that this should not be the case and that someone is to blame. We then lash out in annoyance and frustration or give up in anger and resentment. Neither approach is productive or likely to produce the change outcomes we desire. Mindful leadership is about *expecting the expected.* It involves not being caught out by conditions and problems that, on reflection, we should not be surprised by.

Think About It

Have you ever found yourself in a situation where you can clearly identify a problem, but others seem unable to see it? Have you ever made suggestions and then wondered if anyone heard you? Have you ever felt frustrated by a lack of genuine leadership from those in authority? Have you found your methods and actions frustrated by the lack of workable knowledge? Have you ever thought you put things in place and received agreement from others, but things just don't get done? Instead, everything seems to stall or bog down. Welcome to the gaps in leadership, practice and power!

How might you use Figure 7.2, Mind the Gap(s) to inspire reflection and discussion on potential gaps in the leadership support, practical knowledge or the power required to realize the plans? Consider your emotional preparedness and resilience in acknowledging and working with and on these gaps, as well as your skills and expertise in managing such challenges in practice. What steps might you take to develop your capabilities in these areas further?

Figure 7.3 Mind the Slope.

Individuals and organizations have embedded frames, established expectations and routine patterns for denying anything that challenges these frames and expectations. Overly rational views of organizations systematically underestimate the time, costs and difficulties of effectively bringing about successful transitions. The father of change management, Kurt Lewin, recommended working with people to identify and overcome such barriers (Burnes, 2020; Lewin, 1999). Recognizing and removing the substantial barriers to change is more effective than 'pushing' an agenda while ignoring these conditions. How to achieve this is probably the central change question.

Radical change is routinely hindered by what has been described as 'dynamic conservatism', 'structural inertia' or a reaction against the losses by 'creative destruction'. Although we like to think of ourselves as innovative and progressive, and we may even commit ourselves seriously to the task, we're often reluctant to change what we're used to. British author G.K. Chesterton captured this dilemma nicely, 'New roads, new ruts' (see Chesterton, 2024 [1923], p. 2). We all know the feeling of being stuck in a rut.

The experience of facing these barriers can create a feeling that change is an uphill battle, as in Figure 7.3, Mind the Slope.

In their analysis of 'predictable surprises', Bazerman and Watkins (2004) point to several biases – self-serving psychological, organizational and political – that hinder our ability to recognize the potential disasters caused by these barriers (see Badham and Santiago, 2023, p.4). These biases include deeply rooted issues such as prioritizing short-term thinking and a tendency to favour evidence that supports existing beliefs. Additionally, the fragmentation, sludge and narrow viewpoints created by silos and hierarchies, along with the political biases stemming from established self-interests, power imbalances and fears of speaking out, further contribute to this problem.

Our inability to effectively address these issues stems from four embedded biases in our organizational culture. These include a preference for analytical thinking over emotional understanding (using the head over listening to the heart). A focus on creative design over practical implementation. An emphasis on developing strategy over ensuring execution. A tendency to prioritize reform over achieving results. As captured in Figures 4.3 and 7.3, these biases ('the slope') are rarely straightforward in their nature and impacts. They are part of an organizational world that is more chaotic, in a state of greater disrepair and subject to more ongoing disorganized reconstruction than our overly rational perception of organizations would suggest (see also Figure 1.3, It's Not a Level Playing Field and subsequent analysis).

Think About It

Do you ever find yourself slipping into a naïve belief that the latest 'magic bullet' will solve our pressing issues? Alternatively, do you sometimes retreat in anger or cynical resignation that real or beneficial change is impossible? How might you approach change differently by acknowledging the inevitability of the barriers and biases and learning to work with and navigate through them?

How might you use Figure 7.3 to stimulate reflection and discussion about the importance of being mindful of the biases and barriers to change? How might you develop an ongoing awareness of and attend to such factors? How might you better prepare yourself to accept such conditions?

Figure 7.4 Mind the Complexity.

Being mindful allows leaders to create what Janice Marturano (2014), former CEO of General Mills, calls the 'space to lead'. Leaders who are not mindful often react impulsively to uncertainty and threats, oversimplifying problems and making snap decisions. On the other hand, mindful leaders approach challenges with creativity, care and consideration. In practice, this involves being *reasonable* in the face of irrationalities, retaining a *cosmopolitan* outlook in the face of diversity and difference and being *seriously playful* in the face of the vicissitudes of fate.

To come to terms with the fluidity, uncertainty and complexity of change, leaders must navigate through mindful simplifications and heuristics. They need to establish order in their perceptions, experiences and actions while being sensitive to the fact that they are inherently partial and artificial and must be renewed regularly. In practice, this means working on problems without needing to change our underlying assumptions, as well as exploring different viewpoints when the old ones no longer work. It also means being prepared for and even embracing a life where this is an ongoing activity. This approach embodies what it means to be 'reasonable'. Continuous reflection serves as a reassuring guide amid change and complexity.

Dealing with the tensions and dilemmas of acting in uncertain situations while balancing conflicting viewpoints, principles and performances is challenging. This process begins with the 'head' but doesn't end there – it also involves the heart. It's one thing to be ready to change one's mind; it's quite another to alter how you feel, open yourself up to others and navigate emotional conflict. The stories we tell ourselves and others are rife with prejudice, which makes them so interesting. It is not easy to step outside our own stories, acknowledge the validity of opposing storylines and creatively take into account the emotions and viewpoints of others. In these situations, it's crucial to be aware of and considerate of both their feelings and your own and even to share a sense of humour. This approach embodies what it means to be cosmopolitan.

Finally, having the courage to act under uncertainty, viewing actions as an experiment and learning from mistakes is essential when faced with complex and chaotic conditions. The one thing we can be sure of is that uncertainty is often the norm, and our predictions are likely to be incorrect. To act decisively in these circumstances, we must move beyond 'rigid' or 'fixed' thinking and avoid 'mindless' thought and action. This means being ready to challenge our assumptions and 'think outside the box'. Committing to and developing the ability to embrace this mindset means being 'seriously playful'.

Think About It

If you were to plot your change initiative on a graph with two axes – one representing certainty to uncertainty and the other representing agreement to disagreement – where would you place the objectives and means of any change initiative, you are involved in or examining? As you move towards the uncertainty and disagreement ends, you enter what complexity theorist Ralph Stacey refers to as the 'edge of chaos'. This situation can be stressful.

In Figure 7.4, Mind the Complexity, you can see a leader at this edge, caught between followers seeking answers and the need to take the plunge into uncertain and risky conditions. How well do you think you cope in such scenarios? Consider how you might use Figure 7.4 to encourage reflection and discussion about the intellectual and emotional skills necessary to navigate uncertainty and conflict. Reflect on how you and others have handled similar situations in the past and think about how you can continue to develop these skills in the future.

Chapter 7 Self-Test

Select the <u>one best answer</u> that completes the statements below. There are several 'half-truths' in the other options to choose from. These capture something important but are misleading if taken too far. The 'correct answers' are in Appendix 1. If your answer is incorrect, you might reflect on how it may be 'half-right' but 'half-wrong'.

1. **Being mindful of the J-curve means**
   - A. accepting an inevitable 'valley of death'.
   - B. ensuring motivation and productivity always improve during change.
   - C. expecting and handling a likely downturn in motivation and productivity.
   - D. focusing on the endpoint of change, not getting caught up on the journey.
2. **The gaps we have to be mindful of are**
   - A. problems only created by a failure to adopt best practice change management.
   - B. challenges we have to be aware of, focus attention on and genuinely accept as a reality of change,
   - C. gaps between what we want to do and what we must do.
   - D. traps we inevitably fall into.
3. **The three change gaps lead to**
   - A. shortfalls in leadership, knowledge and power to be expected and addressed.
   - B. inevitably overpromising and under-delivering change outcomes.
   - C. knowing how to achieve change but knowing that success is impossible.
   - D. overcoming irrational resistance by lashing out in frustration and anger.
4. **As an uphill battle, successful change**
   - A. has to be 'pushed' to be achieved.
   - B. requires us to identify and vanquish irrational resistance.
   - C. is an effortful and thankless journey.
   - D. works with people and conditions to create a 'pull' for change.
5. **As a sloped playing field, the change terrain is**
   - A. biased towards considering the 'heart' rather than the 'head'.
   - B. a design challenge in planning and creating a smooth transition.
   - C. a strategic challenge to be addressed through better planning.
   - D. is a predictably chaotic, uncertain and conflictual implementation challenge.
6. **Operating on the 'edge of chaos' means**
   - A. change programmes are inherently unmanageable.
   - B. accepting and working with irreducible uncertainty, diversity and risk.
   - C. we can only succeed by eliminating chaos.
   - D. focusing on creating reassuring narratives of being in control.

8 Mobilizing Leadership

One thing is to be mindful of the challenges of creating a productive change cycle. It is quite another to be willing and able to mobilise energy and resources to address these challenges. At the heart of effective change leadership lies an enthusiasm and capability for creatively mobilizing oneself and others to 'get things done' and 'make things happen'. In this chapter, you will learn what is required to become such a leader, the nature and role of political entrepreneurship, the significance of establishing and maintaining coalitions and the critical importance of mobilizing oneself.

As we have learned, there are biases and barriers to change. It's far from being a level playing field. We love the old joke about the couple driving through Ireland who stop to ask a farmer the way to Cork. His reply was timeless, 'If I were going to go to Cork, I wouldn't start from here!' As human beings, we are forced to embark on our change journey despite unwanted, and often unexpected, biases and barriers to change. And we either become better at dealing with them or not!

Ideally, we'd have all the time, resources and support necessary for a productive change cycle. They're often missing. If we ignore this problem, what people 'normally' do to get things done can be a recipe for disaster. We get the outcomes that 'normally' happen, which is the frequent failure of many change enterprises.

Why do we fail to 'get' this? Well, we have been schooled into thinking that organizations are rational enterprises, that goals and purposes, rituals and routines, are there for very good reasons. We assume that change initiatives have been sensibly planned and that agents and recipients of change will act reasonably to deliver outcomes. We then become frustrated and angry when individuals and organizations act in what we perceive to be blinkered, counter-productive, irrational and self-serving ways. Becoming a leader requires appreciating and working with these conditions to achieve outcomes.

This does not mean abandoning the ethos and techniques of the rational manager. Nor is it entirely possible. Even for those fully aware of

DOI: 10.4324/9781032629971-13

the need for leadership, it is difficult to remove altogether our expectations that people and institutions *will* and *should* behave rationally and strategically. The ideals of rational management are also valuable for directing attention to the importance of using logic and evidence in decision-making, establishing formal roles and responsibilities for delivering outcomes and creating, monitoring and enforcing plans. What it fails to do, however, is provide guidance and support on how to handle the psychological biases and uncertainties of real-world decision-making; recognize and work with the informal and political nature of how things get done; and accept the evolving, speculative and contested nature of strategies, blueprints and schedules for improvement.

Figure 8.1 Becoming a Leader.

A leader must move from a fixed and rigid rational manager mentality to a flexible and growth-oriented mindset. While rational management has its place, it is essential to be ready to address the additional leadership challenges as they arise. This shift means moving beyond the traditional rigid rational manager mindset, with all its comforts and apprehensiveness, and fostering a growth mindset prepared to work on leadership capabilities, even if they are not well developed – *yet*! It requires the exercise of discipline and energetic resourcefulness. Discipline in not letting our misleading expectations derail us and resourcefulness in mobilizing energy and resources to exercise real-world influence.

Think About It

When your expectations of people behaving rationally and responsibly have been disappointed, how proactive have you been in addressing this by using power and influence to persuade and motivate them to act as needed? What steps have you taken to enhance your ability to manage yourself and others when faced with frustrating obstacles and unexpected challenges in implementing change? What prevents you from further developing your skills or feeling inspired to be more effective?

How might you use Figure 8.1, Becoming a Leader, to foster reflection and discussion around your default assumptions and abilities as a manager, which can often be counterproductive? Consider what guides, supports, and inspires you to become more effective. Reflect on the dynamic body language, toolkit, and positive demeanour of the 'becoming' figure versus the passive, hands-behind-the-back stance of the 'being' figure. Discuss whether these stereotypes resonate with you and what it takes to cultivate the qualities of the human 'becoming.'

Figure 8.2 Take a Chance.

In *The Prince*, Machiavelli (2005, p.76/7) observes,

'There is nothing more difficult to execute, nor more dubious of success, nor more dangerous to administer than to introduce new political orders. For the one who introduces them has as his enemies all those who profit from the old order, and he has only lukewarm defenders in all those who might profit from the new order.'

He might have added the resistance we might encounter from those comfortable with established certainties and fixed in their ways, as well as the confounding energy-sapping uncertainty about the likelihood of success and how to achieve it, which is the bane of those trying to bring about change.

Creative, resilient and resourceful entrepreneurialism is essential for those seeking to bring about change in such circumstances. Operating under uncertainty and in conflict situations, 'taking the plunge' may be exciting but is often insecure and stressful. A flexible, growth-oriented and positive mindset is crucial in such conditions. The proactive exercise of influence has long been recognized as an important component in personal achievement and success, as highlighted in celebrated works from Dale Carnegie's *How to Win Friends and Influence People*, through Norman Vincent Peale's *The Power of Positive Thinking* to Stephen Covey's *Seven Habits of Highly Effective People* and *The Eighth Habit.* (see Buchanan and Badham, 1999, 2008, 2020). This positive orientation aligns with contemporary enthusiasm for positive psychology, appreciative inquiry and aspirational discourse, as well as the emerging recognition of change made by 'corporate rebels', 'positive deviants' and 'rebels with talent'.

The entrepreneurial mobilization of energy and resources for change is essential in addressing the gaps, barriers, biases, and complexities identified in the previous chapter. It includes skilful opportunity recognition – spotting gaps or opportunities that can be exploited for a change – gathering and allocating additional resources, ongoing advocacy and persuasion, adept political and cultural manoeuvring, constant networking and relationship building, creative negotiating and conflict resolution, as well as enduring persistence and adaptability.

Think About It

In Figure 8.2, Take a Chance, note the 'Uncertainty' signpost highlighting the enterprise's unknown nature and the added risk of danger from storms and lightning in the distance. Observe the feet-stuck-in-the-mud pull back from those not 'on board' and the pilot's look of doubt and concern as he seeks to get more power from the engine. In preparing for change, how much time and thought do you put into surfacing and addressing the assumptions, uncertainties and fears likely to hold back others (and yourself)? How much time do you spend on acquiring a power base to 'power the engine' to enable you to bring about change in the face of concerns and opposition, i.e. collecting political information, developing and applying interpersonal skills, creating good working relationships and establishing and promoting your credibility and track record?

How might you use Figure 8.2 to encourage reflection and discussion on the fears and reticence that hold people back? Consider how an entrepreneurial mindset and strategic thinking can help generate the energy and resources to address or overcome obstacles. Reflect on whom you think might exhibit a tendency to pull back, as illustrated in the figure, and use the uncertainty sign and stormy imagery to spark conversations about the insecurities and risk aversion they may experience. Use the 'engine' metaphor, along with the pilot's concern, as a starting point for discussing the power and mindset required to conquer these challenges.

Figure 8.3 Build a Coalition.

One person cannot single-handedly bring about change. No matter how energetic, charismatic, visionary and forceful they may be, far more is required. Self-proclaimed 'Lone Rangers' are rarely successful on their own. Even the reluctant Wolverine learns to unite with the wise-cracking Deadpool to save their world(s)!

Any significant endeavour requires a committed coalition. It needs more than the will of heroic innovators or change agents. It involves forging a collective will, an effective coalition of supporters, enthusiasts and champions. Purposeful mission-driven coalitions provide the resources, energy, and intelligence necessary to effectively prepare for change, initiate it, implement it and stabilize it.

At each stage, creating and maintaining effective coalitions requires personal adaptability and political nous. It is an iterative process of creating and recreating agendas and mobilizing and remobilizing support around them. In traditional project leadership terms, this involves establishing and maintaining the support of three key groups: a 'steering group' (to provide and sustain strategic resources and legitimacy), a 'working team' (to provide energy, resourcefulness and persistence in addressing challenges and keeping up momentum); and an 'invisible network' (to call upon for additional advice and assistance as needed to overcome obstacles. Navigating these groups requires operating at the 'speed of trust', balancing commitments, and managing competing coalitions, all critical challenges for securing and maintaining their support. Achieving change also involves mobilizing a broader 'volunteer army' ready to face the risks and challenges of dismantling the status quo.

A key component of this enterprise is creating and maintaining a coherent and inspiring change narrative. The stories surrounding change initiatives emerge from a contested terrain. Both agents and recipients of change may encounter and, to varying degrees, subscribe to quite different narratives of events. These narratives can include heroic tales of positive progress, villainous stories of negative regression, narratives of stability that question the extent of change and tales of chaos and confusion. Each frames those initiating change and those impacted by it as heroic innovators, irresponsible villains, misguided individuals, courageous resisters or tragic, powerless victims. In this context, creating plausible and authentic storylines that are both inspiring and realistic is vital for countering critics and fostering coalitions and support.

Change consultants often recommend capturing and celebrating 'small wins' to sustain momentum. This is part of generating and sustaining stories that build confidence, maintain enthusiasm, foster resilience and combat change fatigue and cynicism.

How often have you leapt into a 'just do it' approach to a change without considering whether you have the power and influence necessary to achieve it? How well did that go? What steps can you take to define, build and maintain a coalition with the skills, energy, and resources necessary to bring about change? How do you 'sell' the change in a way that considers where people are currently and makes a compelling intellectual and emotional case for involvement in change?

Think About It

How effective is the approach pictured in Figure 8.3, Build a Coalition? It features a confident, arms-crossed senior manager at the head of the table offering prescriptions in formal meetings to a rather passive and expressionless group. In what ways does the senior manager's stance reflect the important insight that 'actions speak louder than words'?

How might you use Figure 8.3 to stimulate discussion and reflection on the need for informal as well as formal methods for establishing and sustaining momentum in creating and sustaining supportive ***coalitions*** *and* ***narratives****?*

Figure 8.4 Mobilize Yourself.

Mobilizing yourself goes beyond being mindful of the challenges of change to proactively mobilizing the energy and resources required to overcome them. The skill and will to mobilize energy, support and resources are crucial to change capability.

Developing these skills and acting in this way is personally challenging. As one senior change manager said, 'Change always requires you to put in that extra bit to ensure things get done.' That 'extra bit' can be exhausting and risky for the enterprise. It's essential, therefore, that you're able to mobilize yourself. So, as a general rule, do whatever you can to pursue changes that align with your values and enhance your career. Your resilience, persistence, and fate will depend upon it.

Being proactive in change involves seriously attending to your motivations. Proactivity is encouraged by 'can do' motivations (e.g., feelings of self-efficacy, sense of feasibility, belief risks are not too great), 'reason to' motivations (e.g., activities are intrinsically enjoyable, outcomes contribute to important goals, feeling responsible, goals aligning with existing and future desired identity and purposes), and 'energized to' motivations (e.g., 'hot' feelings of enthusiasm and inspiration at work). Shaping and adapting the change and/or your role to enhance such motivations can be crucial in sustaining yourself over time.

Finally, what ultimately justifies the frustrations, risks and stresses of making real change happen? For some, it is career success; for some, caring for their colleagues; for others, it is just being responsible and doing one's job. In addition to such motives, however, there is a deeper personal agenda. Thinking about change issues sensitizes us to the real-life challenges we all face. Understanding and handling your emotions and those of others gives you greater control over your life. It also improves your ability to forge enduring and meaningful relationships. Developing your ability to act confidently and creatively in conflict and uncertainty is an enduring source of satisfaction, development and success. It is common for those involved in meaningful and challenging change to say, 'I will never be the same again' and go on to new and challenging careers.

Think About It

Mobilizing yourself to become a leader is an ongoing developmental challenge that requires working on your capabilities and mindset. Figure 8.4, Mobilize Yourself, illustrates this concept by depicting gym characters with various levels of fitness striving to improve their fitness. Some individuals are preparing – getting dressed and bringing in weights – while others are engaging in different exercise methods. A coach, inspirational messaging, and fitness trackers are present to support them.

How might you use Figure 8.4 to stimulate discussion and reflection on how to support yourself and others in developing your capabilities and motivation to be proactive and energetic in driving change? Consider the varying levels of capability and the importance of supportive methods and people in this process.

Chapter 8 Self-Test

Select the <u>three best answers</u> **that complete the statements below**. There are several 'half-truths' in the other options to choose from. These capture something important but are misleading if taken too far. The 'correct answers' are in Appendix 1. If your answer is incorrect, you might reflect on how it may be 'half-right' but 'half-wrong'.

1. **Becoming a leader means**

   A. abandoning rational management.
   B. working with psychological biases, organizational politics and uncertain fluidity of change.

C. crafting and recrafting a vision and agenda to get people on board and maintain their commitment.
D. accepting the biases and barriers that hold back change and being disciplined and energetic in handling them.

2. **Political entrepreneurship is essential because we need to**

A. use informal persuasion as well as formal authority to motivate those involved in change.
B. put ourselves first and look after our careers.
C. develop a power base for bringing about change.
D. adopt a flexible, growth-oriented, positive approach is necessary for navigating uncertainty and conflict.

3. **Building coalitions involves**

A. creating alliances with those working on and affected by change.
B. establishing and integrating steering groups, working teams and invisible networks.
C. creating a project team with a clear agenda and schedule.
D. personal adaptability and political nous in creating and sustaining networks for change.

4. **A coherent and challenging change narrative**

A. balances plausibility with inspiration.
B. is required to counter nay-sayers and negative stories about the change and those promoting it.
C. helps create and sustain confidence and enthusiasm in the face of opposition.
D. blames resistors for their irrational opposition.

5. **Mobilizing yourself for change**

A. involves ensuring or developing your ability to mobilize others.
B. is a luxury as the success of change depends on others.
C. includes paying attention to project success aligning with your values and career aspirations.
D. includes being able to act confidently and creatively in conflict and uncertainty.

6. **Being proactive in change is enhanced by**

A. purposeful 'reason to' motivations.
B. confident 'can do' motivations.
C. emotions that energize you to bring about change.
D. ensuring you are not exhausted by change and do not take risks.

9 Lightness of Being

In an emotional voice, the Vice President of a multinational IT firm announced, 'It is all very well to be adaptive, mindful and able to handle complexity, but we are all going to be out on stress relief!' When we mentioned the importance of a 'lightness of being', she was happy, enthused and wanted to learn more. This chapter provides you with a light introduction to the subject. You will learn the importance of riding the wave in change surfing, enjoying the ride with a lightness of thought, heart and touch and being seriously playful and remembering to laugh.

Figure 9.1 Ride the Wave.

Conventional change management operates under the assumption that acquiring knowledge of change dynamics and applying appropriate

DOI: 10.4324/9781032629971-14

methods, processes and tools will ensure the desired outcomes. While it acknowledges that there are issues in managing change, it seeks and is confident of being able to 'tame' them and find 'solutions'. It is the classic belief in a 'magic bullet' approach.

However, just as therapists caution against counsellors attempting to 'fix' their clients' problems, a similar issue arises with this 'fix-it' change mentality. Not everything can be 'fixed'. Change often involves enduring contradictions, challenges, tensions and dilemmas and complex 'wicked' problems that we must learn to accept, endure and navigate. An excessive commitment to a 'fix-it' approach can undermine the change process itself. Individuals adopting such an approach tend to experience higher levels of stress, disappointment, frustration and burnout, leading to counterproductive 'fight or flight' responses.

Becoming a change leader requires a change mindset that transcends the rational manager's rigid 'fix it' mentality. It involves accepting, working with and artfully adapting to the conditions and realities of change.

Think About It

The metaphor of 'change surfing' directs us towards the importance of style, balance and achievement in navigating the turbulent conditions we face while creating a successful 'ride'. Figure 9.1, Ride the Wave, adds two additional images to this metaphor, emphasizing the challenging yet rewarding nature of this endeavour.

Firstly, the wave is inspired by 'The Great Wave off Kanagawa', a print by the Japanese artist Hokusai. This artwork symbolizes the threatening, and powerful claw-like nature of a giant wave, reminding us that change is rarely smooth sailing. Secondly, the surfer's board is represented as a 'Red Pill'. This refers to the more realistic, profound, yet often disturbing view of the world chosen by Keanu Reeves's character Leo in '*The Matrix*'. He opts for this perspective over the comfortable but deceptive view of those who take the 'blue pill' (see Chapter 1, Figure 1.1, The Box).

Understanding and influencing change requires us to go beyond conventional illusions and deepen our appreciation of what change entails and demands. Although this exploration can be uncomfortable at times, there is a sense of satisfaction and success in moving past simplistic and bland orthodoxies.

How might you use Figure 9.1 to inspire discussion and reflection on 'riding the wave of change' as a metaphor for working with the realities of change? In what ways does the use of the Great Wave and the Red Pill illustrate the threatening nature of some of these conditions and the associated risks, as well as the satisfaction and benefits that can arise from facing up to and working with these challenges?

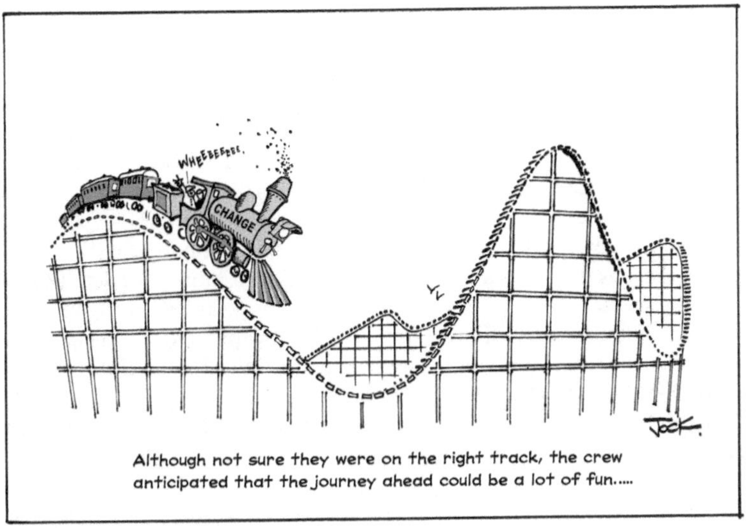

Figure 9.2 Enjoy the Ride.

As formally recognized or self-designated 'agents of change', we often find ourselves caught up in a managerial mystique that believes organizational life should be efficient and orderly. We tend to see ourselves and our projects as heroic agents or saviours on a grand march to salvation. This mindset leads us to expect and strive for a productive and harmonious journey. Leaders proclaim it, clients demand it, employees expect it, consultants advise it, academics study it and we come to impose it upon ourselves.

Filled with expectations that people and processes ought to be more rational than they often are, we frequently lash out unproductively in frustration and anger, particularly when under pressure. We often end up 'pushing' change in ways that only heighten resistance and opposition.

The result? Suffering and burnout – in both ourselves and others – as we lose all sense of what is realistically attainable. Preoccupied with such problems, we are less likely to think strategically and less inclined to focus on what is possible and achievable in the current circumstances.

When we change our mindset and free ourselves from this burden, we can respond far better (and even enjoy) the predictable and unpredictable irrationalities of managing and leading change. It involves adopting a bearable 'lightness of being' that transcends mere 'lightness of thought' to include a 'lightness of heart' and a 'lightness of touch'. Each of these elements is essential as our reflexive response to the frustrations and challenges of change is an embodied one. While intellectual awareness is crucially important, it must be accompanied by emotional intelligence and practical wisdom to combat our habitual responses.

Muhammed Ali, arguably one of the world's greatest boxers of all time, famously promised boxing fans that in his fights, he'd 'Float like a butterfly, sting like a bee…' (see Badham and Santiago, 2023, p. 271). In contrast, most people tend to float more like bees and sting like butterflies!

In his book *The Unbearable Lightness of Being*, Milan Kundera (2009) valued the ability to free ourselves from our overly serious, overly rational assumptions, plans and duties. However, he also pointed out the anxiety and insecurity that can arise from this freedom, as we must craft a meaningful life beyond the comforts of convention.

How can we develop a lightness of thought, holding our assumptions and ideas lightly without losing faith in reason? How might we retain a lightness of heart, acknowledging the partial and relative nature of our personal feelings and prejudices, without losing our bearings and a sense of purpose? How can we maintain a lightness of touch, viewing the actions we invest in as experiments without loss of enthusiasm and energy?

Think About It

Figure 9.2, Enjoy the Ride depicts joyful passengers on a rollercoaster to illustrate the uncertain change journey, characterized by its thrilling ups and downs. It reflects the anxiety of not knowing if one is on the 'right track' while also capturing the excitement of anticipating a fun experience. Embracing such a ride on the change rollercoaster, rather than being overwhelmed by fear at the challenging moments ahead, requires a certain mindset both mentally and physically.

How might you use Figure 9.2 to stimulate discussion and reflection on coping with and enjoying the emotional rollercoaster of change? Additionally, how can the idea of relaxing and enjoying the rollercoaster ride inspire questions about the importance and benefits of maintaining a lightness of thought, heart and touch?

Figure 9.3 Remember to Laugh.

Our proposal is that you adopt a seriously playful approach to change. 'Seriously playful' combines two seemingly contradictory qualities: seriousness and playfulness. This approach to change embodies a mindset that balances light-hearted, fun, spontaneity and creativity with deep purpose, commitment and focus. It encourages us to take our work seriously while also allowing space for joy and innovation.

Being 'seriously playful' in the context of change means bringing enthusiasm and purpose to our tasks while maintaining a strong focus on our goals. This approach blends joyfulness with depth; the playful aspect enhances creativity and reduces stress and rigidity, ultimately making us more effective.

The phrase 'remember to laugh' carries a dual meaning. It reflects a somewhat tragic frustration and acceptance of situations not working out as expected while also encouraging a comic appreciation of our own and others' foolishness for thinking things could be different. Incongruities often prompt laughter, and we believe it's better to laugh than to cry – especially when faced with the chaos and hypocrisy that can accompany change.

Laughter is a source of relief, helping us cope with the stress of trying to meet unrealistic expectations. Additionally, it fosters social bonding through shared enjoyment of the absurdities we encounter. For instance, it helps to highlight the arrogance of those who threaten punishment for noncompliance, reminding us of the ultimate lack of control over such situations.

Think About It

Figure 9.3, Remember to Laugh, presents a somewhat ironic illustration of the lightness of being. On one level, it contrasts the somewhat perplexed expression of the manager holding the traditional change proposal with the contagious mirth of those who are too aware of the frequent absurdities in the analysis and expectations. On another level, the manager seems to mistakenly interpret this joyous ridicule as acceptance and enjoyment. However, in doing so, he unintentionally conveys a truth – it is essential for those involved in change to maintain a sense of humour when navigating their own fallibilities and the foolishness of others in the change process.

How might you use Figure 9.3 to spark discussion and reflection on improving communication and understanding between the manager presenting the change proposal and those responding to it? How can you transform this situation into a platform for creative problem-solving, thereby preventing it from devolving into conflict or avoiding genuine opinions? Can you find a way to get everyone constructively laughing?

Chapter 9 Self-Test

Select the <u>one best answer</u> that completes the statements below. There are several 'half-truths' in the other options to choose from. These capture something important but are misleading if taken too far. The 'correct answers' are in Appendix 1. If your answer is incorrect, you might reflect on how it may be 'half-right' but 'half-wrong'.

1. **Bringing about change is**

   A. something that requires fixing.
   B. an absurd endeavour we should simply laugh about.
   C. an impossible task we need to accept and live with.
   D. potentially rewarding, requiring resilience and a sense of humour.

2. **Change surfing involves**

   A. accepting and using the winds and tides of change.
   B. creating plans and sticking to them.
   C. allowing yourself to go with the flow.
   D. ensuring you never go below the surface.

3. **Enjoying the ride means**

   A. pushing for a change that delights you.
   B. being prepared and flexible in the face of ups and downs.
   C. relying on people to do the right and intelligent thing.
   D. looking after yourself first.

4. **A lightness of being requires**

   A. floating like a bee and stinging like a butterfly.
   B. alcohol and drugs.
   C. a lightness of thought, heart and touch.
   D. light-hearted frivolity and avoiding conflict and contention.

5. **Being seriously playful means**

   A. being playful and responsible, light-hearted and committed.
   B. enjoying everything about change.
   C. removing stupidity, irrationality and chaos.
   D. not taking things seriously.

6. **Humour and laughter are for**

   A. the superficial and irresponsible.
   B. those who are cynical and resigned.
   C. those avoiding taking change seriously.
   D. enjoyment, relief and camaraderie.

Section 3

Key Takeaways and Resources

Key Takeaways

Chapter 7. Mindful Leadership

- **Be prepared for the dip**. Be ready for the tension between the rhetoric of change and the realities of the 'J-curve' to avoid a crash into 'Death Valley'.
- **Be mindful of the gaps**. Be aware of, focus on and fully accept the challenges created by leadership, practice and power gaps in change.
- **Work with the slope and the biases**. Adjust to and work with the sloped playing field created by biases towards the head over the heart, design over implementation, strategy over execution and reform over results.
- **Have the courage to work on the 'edge of chaos'**. Be reasonable, cosmopolitan and seriously playful when faced with uncertainty and conflict on the 'edge of chaos'.

Chapter 8. Mobilizing Leadership

- **Develop yourself as a leader**. While conventional management capabilities are important, embark on the ongoing developmental process of going beyond them to become a leader.
- **Enhance your entrepreneurial qualities**. Recognize and improve your entrepreneurial mindset and skills. Learn to manage cognitive biases and emotional insecurities. Embrace creativity, resilience and political savvy to gather the energy and resources needed to overcome obstacles.
- **Build and sustain momentum**. Create the momentum necessary to overcome challenges by forming powerful and influential alliances. Craft compelling change narratives that inspire confidence and resonate with others.
- **Mobilize yourself**. Cultivate proactive motivation to drive change and develop the skills and determination to mobilize others effectively.

DOI: 10.4324/9781032629971-15

Chapter 9. Lightness of Being

- **Ride the wave**. Let go of an uptight 'fix-it' mentality. Embrace the realities of change and learn to work with the conditions rather than against them.
- **Assume a lightness of being**. Develop a balanced lightness of thought, a heart filled with appreciation and a creative, experimental approach to challenges.
- **Be seriously playful**. Approach your goals for change with a balanced attitude that combines seriousness and playfulness. This lightheartedness can boost creativity and enhance resilience.
- **Cultivate constructive laughter**. Focus on cultivating shared humour, using laughter to strengthen bonds rather than to ridicule. This encourages a mutual recognition of absurdities and promotes a collaborative search for solutions.

Resources

- *Ironies of Organizational Change*
  Act 3 Leadership of Change
  Ch. 6 'Knowing-Doing Gaps', Ch. 7 'Paradoxes of Change' & Ch. 8 'Ironies of Change', pp. 165–261, Epilogue, pp. 262–276.
- *Coursera Program*
  Week 6 Leading Change: Mindful and Mobilising
  Five short video lectures, one reading and one test.
- *Short Change: An Introduction to Managing Change*
  'Ch. 3 'Mindful Change', Ch. 4 'Mobilising Change', Appendix: 'Principles of Change Management', and Further Reading.
- *Power, Politics and Organizational Change*
  First Edition (1999) Ch. 4 'Men Behaving Badly', Ch. 5 'The Entrepreneurial Hero' & Ch. 6 'The Politics of Failure and the Failure of Politics', pp. 99–178.
  Second Edition (2008) Ch. 4 'Men Behaving Badly', Ch. 6 'Entrepreneurial Heroes' & Ch. 7 'The Good, the Bad and the Ugly' (pp. 115–149, 173–211, 212–245).
  Third Edition (2020) Ch. 5 'Cutting the Bullshit', Ch. 6 'Telling Tales', Ch. 7 'Speaking Up', pp. 155–222.
- *Reimagining Change website* (www.reimaginingchange.com)
  Supplementary materials are on our website to support Ch. 7 8 in *Ironies of Organizational Change*. These can be accessed by clicking on 'Go to Online Resources' on the home page and then clicking on '3 Book Chapters 7-8' and/or '4 Referenced Book Materials'. These may be of interest as background.

Conclusion

This book adopts a seriously playful approach to managing and leading change. It does so in form and content.

The cartoons have been designed to communicate key insights in fun and entertaining ways. They use humour and parody to entertain and disturb complacency, prick arrogance and debunk illusions. The playbook opens up a world of creative and stimulating images to inspire reflection, fuel discussion, help you get out of your head and break any counterproductive habits you might possess.

Figure 10.1 Reimagine Change.

DOI: 10.4324/9781032629971-16

The sections that order and integrate the cartoons and chapters provide you with three fundamental building blocks for reimagining change:

1. **Redefine the change problem**. Be prepared to acknowledge that we struggle with managing change well, and there are valid reasons for this. To keep this in mind and guide your actions, reimagine organizations as Icebergs, the change journey as a Rollercoaster ride, and reinvent yourself as a Leader.
2. **Create a productive change cycle**. Reimagine the conventional view of change management as an ongoing and iterative cycle of creating maps, donning masks and deploying mirrors. These images better capture the partial and tentative nature of 'plans', the interactive performance of 'doing' as the exercise of influence, and the importance of understanding and addressing the selective, biased and contested nature of reflective checks or 'evaluations.
3. **Become a leader of change**. As an agent of change, you are both a change manager and a leader. As a manager, you establish the foundations for a rational plan-do-check cycle. As a leader, you reimagine this framework as a 'maps-masks-mirrors' cycle, are mindful of the complexities and barriers that undermine this cycle and are ready to mobilize energy and resources to overcome them. Given our tendency to default to rational management, developing the necessary discipline becomes an ongoing personal development process.

Change management is the discipline of influencing oneself and others to achieve a specific purpose. The 5M framework supports this discipline by focusing on creating a productive change cycle through the mindful mobilization of maps, masks and mirrors. We hope you find the cartoons engaging, each chapter helpful and informative and the sections valuable as personal guides. For those interested in exploring these ideas and approaches further, follow up on the additional in-depth resources provided at the end of each section.

Good luck on the journey!

Appendix

Self-Test Answers

For each chapter self-test, award yourself 1 point for each correct answer, for a maximum score of six points per chapter self-test. WARNING!! Ensure you read the instructions carefully. Some chapter self-tests ask you to pick two or three correct answers for each question. Give yourself one point if you get all the correct answers to one question, and no more! Good Luck!

On Scoring

- **0–2**: The good news is that there is genuine scope for improving your life, personally and at work. Consider the simple rules, however uncomfortable at first, and see how you go. Remember: don't let the initial discomfort dim your enthusiasm. We promise you, you have a world to win!
- **3–4**: Your approach to change is mature. There is, however, work to be done to improve, and it looks as if you are entirely up to it. Check on where you scored high and low, think about what this means, and work out what you might do about it.
- **5–6**: Congrats. You have a proactive change mindset – IF you answered the questions honestly! If you scored 5, look at where you stumbled and think how you might improve.

Chapter 1 Self-Test Answers

1. D
2. C
3. C
4. B
5. D
6. A

7 Mindful Leadership

Leading change is the exercise of influence required to keep a productive change cycle going. It has two key components that complement each other: being *mindful* of the gaps, barriers and complexity that challenge any change enterprise and *mobilizing* energy and resources to address them. It combines an awareness of the challenges of change (combining reflexivity, wariness, prudence and care) with enthusiasm for 'getting things done' (creatively, energetically and positively mobilizing oneself and others). In this chapter, you will discover what is involved in being mindful of three fundamental challenges: knowing-doing *gaps, barriers* created by inherent biases against change and *complexities* of handling uncertainty, tension and chaos.

There is an inherent and fundamental tension in modern organizations. We want and need to change, yet we find it very difficult in practice. Organizations need to innovate and change to survive and thrive. They also need to proclaim and demonstrate to all their stakeholders that this is what they are doing. Still, it seems as if organizations are perfectly designed to ensure otherwise. Established frames of thought, embedded habits and vested interests all act against our aspirations and strategies for realizing change.

As a result, organizations proclaim and are called upon to lead change efficiently and effectively. Yet what is commonly recognized and regularly experienced is its mishandling. Misleading change occurs if this tension is not fully understood or properly addressed.

Mindful leadership is consciously *aware* of the gaps, barriers and complexities that make the change journey challenging. It is disciplined in focusing and sustaining *attention* on the challenges they create and how to adapt. Finally, it is an *acceptance* of the challenges. This involves expecting and preparing for them and meeting friction and opposition with equanimity, sympathy, and, where necessary, compassion.

In support of such an approach, Figure 7.1, The Dip illustrates what is known as the 'J-curve' of change. The J-curve captures the nature of

DOI: 10.4324/9781032629971-12

Chapter 2 Self-Test Answers

1. C
2. B
3. D
4. D
5. B
6. A

Chapter 3 Self-Test Answers

1. C, D
2. B, D
3. B, D
4. B, C
5. B, C
6. A, D

Chapter 4 Self-Test Answers

1. B, D
2. A, C
3. A, B
4. B, C
5. A, D
6. C, D

Chapter 5 Self-Test Answers

1. A, B
2. A, C
3. B, C
4. C, D
5. A, B
6. B, D

Chapter 6 Self-Test Answers

1. D
2. A
3. C
4. D
5. B
6. B

Chapter 7 Self-Test Answers

1. C
2. B
3. A
4. D
5. D
6. B

Chapter 8 Self-Test Answers

1. B, C, D
2. A, C, D
3. A, B, D
4. A, B, C
5. A, C, D
6. A, B, C

Chapter 9 Self-Test Answers

1. D
2. A
3. B
4. C
5. A
6. D

References

Badham, R., 2022, James March and the poetry of leadership. *Journal of Management History*, *28*(1), 46–65.

Badham, R.J. and Santiago, B.M., 2023, *Ironies of Organizational Change: Introduction to Change Management and Organizational Theory*. Edward Elgar Publishing.

Badham, R., 2014, *Short Change: An Introduction to Managing Change*. Business Perspectives.

Bazerman, M. and Watkins, M., 2004. *Predictable Surprises: The Disasters You Should Have Seen Coming and How to Prevent Them*. Harvard Business School Press.

Borges, J., 1999, On exactitude in science. In J.L. Borges (Ed.) and A. Hurley (Trans.), *Collected Fictions*. Penguin Books.

Buchanan, D. and Badham, R., 1999, *Power, Politics and Organizational Change* (1st ed.). Sage.

Buchanan, D. and Badham, R., 2008, *Power, Politics and Organizational Change* (2nd ed.). Sage.

Buchanan, D. and Badham, R., 2020, *Power, Politics and Organizational Change* (3rd ed.). Sage.

Burnes, B., 2020, The origins of Lewin's three-step model of change. *The Journal of Applied Behavioral Science*, *56*(1), 32–59.

Camus, A., 2023. *The Myth of Sisyphus*. BK Classics.

Chesterton, G.K., (2024), Fads and Fancies [original 1923] In *The GK Chesterton Collection*. Henderson Publishing.

Economist Intelligence Unit, 2011, *Leaders of Change: Companies Prepare for a Stronger Future*. The Economist.

Goffman, E., 2022 [1959], *The Presentation of Self in Everyday Life*. Doubleday.

Inspiring Change, 2024, *Ironies of Organizational Change: Online Resources*. https://reimaginingchange.com (Accessed 9 December 2024).

Korzybski, A., 1933, *Science and Sanity. An Introduction to Non-Aristotelean Systems and General Semantics*. The International Non-Aristotelean Library Pub.

Kundera, M., 2009, *The Unbearable Lightness of Being*. Harper.

Lewin, K., 1999, *The Complete Social Scientist: A Kurt Lewin Reader*. American Psychological Association.

Machiavelli, N., 2005, *The Prince*. Peter Bondanella (Trans.). Oxford University Press

Marturano, J., 2014, *Finding the Space to Lead*. Bloomsbury Press.

Project Management Institute, 2024, *PMI Official Website 'Change Management'*. https://www.pmi.org/search#q=change%20management&sort=relevancy (Accessed 9 December 2024).

Prosci, 2024, *The PROSCI ADKAR Model*. https://www.prosci.com/methodology/adkar (Accessed 9 December 2024).

Shakespeare, W., 1999 [1599], *Julius Caesar*. Arthur Humphreys (Ed.). Oxford University Press.

Weick, K., 1995, *Sense-making in Organizations*. Sage.

Index